Deliciously rebellious,
dangerously blasph[emous]
for your spiritual searc[h]

D0195903

"Do not read this book if you want to continue your spiritual journey via the same well-worn, rutted course. For those who prefer the status quo, beware; this is rebellious, even dangerous, material ahead. To leave known, comfortable paths and head into new realms is unsettling, even scary. For some, introducing humor into the sacred can be like jarring bedrock. But beneath the bedrock lies undiscovered layers of rich, raw materials—natural resources that can transform our very lives."

—FROM THE INTRODUCTION

Have you been lulled into believing that humor is inappropriate or disrespectful in spiritual realms—maybe even blasphemous? If so, ask yourself this: Inappropriate according to whom?

Rev. Susan Sparks, America's only female stand-up comedian with a pulpit, wants you to reconnect with your inherent ability to laugh and satisfy the part of your humanity that yearns for joy. With compelling stories from her life, Rev. Sparks tracks the various ways humor has been revered in ancient cultures and world religious traditions, and explores why humor is rarely included in our images of God. She highlights ways that humor allows us to transcend our isolation and our barriers, and reveals how humor can be the ark that carries us when tragedy hits.

No matter how dormant your joy, Rev. Sparks will help you unpack your fears and reclaim laughter as a spiritual gift. Just try it. You may be surprised.

"Helps us transcend to a higher and better place, no matter what our circumstances. A much needed balm for a world that often forgets how to laugh."
—Saranne Rothberg, CEO, The ComedyCures Foundation;
host, ComedyCures LaughTalk Radio

Also Available

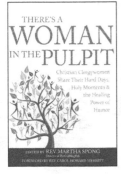

There's a Woman in the Pulpit
Christian Clergywomen Share Their Hard Days, Holy Moments & the Healing Power of Humor
Edited by Rev. Martha Spong; Foreword by Rev. Carol Howard Merritt
Clergywomen explore their holy—and unflinchingly human—moments as they juggle the sometimes isolating expectations from their congregations and the shared realities, graces and humor of everyday life.
6 x 9, 240 pp, Quality PB, 978-1-59473-588-2

God the What?
What Our Metaphors for God Reveal about Our Beliefs in God
By Carolyn Jane Bohler

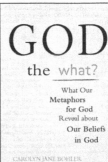

Challenges your common images of God by blowing the lid off conventional God-descriptors. Inspires you to consider a wide range of images of God in order to refine how you imagine God to have and use power, and how God wills and makes divine will happen—or not.
6 x 9, 192 pp, Quality PB, 978-1-59473-251-5

REV. SUSAN SPARKS, the only female comedian in the country with a pulpit, is senior pastor of the historic Madison Avenue Baptist Church in New York City (and the first woman pastor in its 165-year history). She has been featured in *O (The Oprah Magazine)*, the *New York Times*, *USA Today* and on such networks as CBS, ABC and CNN. She is the recipient of an award from Intersections International for her interfaith work to promote justice, reconciliation and peace among diverse communities. Susan is also a professional comedian touring nationally with a stand-up

rabbi and a Muslim comic in the Laugh in Peace Tour. As a cancer survivor, Susan travels the country offering keynotes to survivors and caregivers as well as health-care professionals. Connect with her through her blogs, YouTube channel, newsletter and sermons via www.susansparks.com.

"More than a delightfully written book; it is a Saturday afternoon conversation with a favorite friend at the neighborhood coffee shop. I hope that this is just the first installment in an ongoing Saturday afternoon conversation with a new favorite friend, Susan Sparks."

—**Pam Durso**, executive director, Baptist Women in Ministry

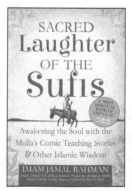
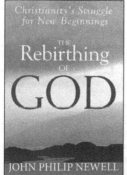

Praise for
Laugh Your Way to Grace:
Reclaiming the Spiritual Power of Humor

"Humor and theology—together? Absolutely! And *Laugh Your Way to Grace* is the blueprint for the relationship. This pioneering book taps ancient wisdom about laughter which we all innately have, but often forget. Susan Sparks reconnects us with this power by reminding us, page by page, that we can chuckle and grin our way toward life abundant."   **—Rev. Dr. Serene Jones,** president,
Union Theological Seminary

"Rev. Susan Sparks shares her own phenomenal journey as she inspires us to enter the laughing space within us all. It is the 'sacred space' where healing, light, forgiveness, love, compassion, creativity, and spiritual connection live."
                        —Dr. Dale V. Atkins, psychologist,
author, media commentator

"When approaching religious matters we are taught to steel our hearts, buttress our minds, and gird our souls because, as all of us are constantly reminded, religion is deathly (or after-deathly) serious. With this moving, smart, spiritual, and *funny* book, Rev. Susan Sparks gives us permission to let the power of humor open up space for new and transforming grace in our religious practice and discourse. The pastoral effect is to liberate the reader from the spiritually deadening shackles that bind us—and smile, chuckle, and laugh out loud our way to redemption."   **—Paul Brandeis Raushenbush,**
religion editor, *Huffington Post*

"I read *Laugh Your Way to Grace* on a day when the weight of the world felt especially heavy on my shoulders. By the time I finished reading and laughing, the burden was lifted, proving Susan Sparks' point: laughter is a spiritual practice that empowers the human heart to fly."   **—Robert D. Black,** producer, *30 Good Minutes*

"In a cynical postmodern world, Susan Sparks recovers the healing art of humor and theological reflection wrapped in story. Rare is it to find one with a deep commitment to the love, justice, and beauty of laughter. The ministry of Susan Sparks has blessed my life and this publication will be a blessing to all who journey with this high priestess of humor and holy reflection."

—**Rev. Otis Moss, III,** pastor,
Trinity United Church of Christ, Chicago

"I laughed. I got chills. Each page is a gem. But most importantly *Laugh Your Way to Grace* reminded me that every moment of laughter, even in some of the most painful times of life, is an act of the holy, an act of God. Knowing this truth, our lives may become a little sweeter, a little lighter, and a lot more fun."

—**Rabbi Sherre Hirsch,** author, *We Plan, God Laughs*

"You could buy this book just for the chapter titles or the great quotes that begin each section—but you would miss the chance to laugh your way to grace…. This is not a book filled with jokes, but with the surprising humor that comes from paying close attention to life. You will discover laughter that is not frivolous, but healing…. When you come to the end of this book you'll want to pass it on to someone who has never imagined laughing on the spiritual path. They will surely thank you."

—**Barbara K. Lundblad,** Joe R. Engle
Professor of Preaching, Union Theological Seminary

"A great read. Humor yourself all the way to spiritual enlightenment. A humorous ride to a zillion and one reasons to invite laughter into your spiritual house."

—**Moshe Cohen,** founder of Clowns Without Borders—USA

Reclaiming the
Spiritual Power of Humor

Laugh
your
way
to
Grace

Rev. Susan Sparks

Walking Together, Finding the Way ®
SKYLIGHT PATHS®
PUBLISHING

Laugh Your Way to Grace:
Reclaiming the Spiritual Power of Humor

Requests to the Publisher for permission should be addressed to Turner Publishing Company, 4507 Charlotte Avenue, Suite 100, Nashville, Tennessee, (615) 255-2665, fax (615) 255-5081, E-mail: submissions@turnerpublishing.com.

Unless otherwise indicated, scripture quotations are from the *New Revised Standard Version Bible*, copyright © 1989 by the Division of Christian Education of the National Council of the Churches of Christ in the USA. Used by permission. All rights reserved.

© 2010 by Susan Sparks

Library of Congress Cataloging-in-Publication Data
Sparks, Susan, 1962–
Laugh your way to grace : reclaiming the spiritual power of humor / Susan Sparks.—
1st quality paperback ed.
p. cm.
Includes bibliographical references.
ISBN 978-1-59473-280-5 (quality pbk. original)
1. Laughter—Religious aspects. 2. Wit and humor—Religious aspects. 3. Religion—Humor. I. Title.
BL65.L3S63 2010
233'.5—dc22

2010015058

ISBN 978-1-59473-343-7 (eBook)

Manufactured in the United States of America
Cover Design: Jenny Buono

Walking Together, Finding the Way®
Published by SkyLight Paths Publishing
An imprint of Turner Publishing Company
www.skylightpaths.com

ISBN 978-1-68336-168-8 (hc)

This book is dedicated to the memory of my parents, Ann and Herb Sparks, two people quick to love and quick to laugh; and to the memory of Dr. Edwina (Wyn) Wright, professor of biblical languages at Union Theological Seminary, a dear friend and a warrior for laughter on the spiritual path.

Contents

PART II What Would Happen If We Laughed?

Acknowledgments

A special word of thanks to all those who helped launch this book, particularly my family and friends who offered endless support; my congregation at Madison Avenue Baptist Church in New York City; SkyLight Paths Publishing and my editor, Marcia Broucek; and most of all to my partner, Toby, my true source of joy.

Introduction

"Humor is not a trick, not jokes. Humor is a presence in the world, like grace, and shines on everyone."
—GARRISON KEILLOR, AUTHOR, STORYTELLER, AND HUMORIST

"You're a *what*?"

After years as a stand-up comedian *and* a minister, that is the number one response I have come to expect.

"*Why*?" is second.

And "you *actually* have a job?" is third.

Of course, I don't blame people. This is not a career path encouraged by most high school counselors or a job you see posted on Craigslist.

When you mention humor and religion in the same breath, most people think of Noah jokes and nun puns. And those are great—at least some of them. But the power of humor on the spiritual path radiates far beyond the realm of punch lines.

Laughter is, in fact, a way of coming at the world. It challenges how we perceive ourselves and our circumstances, it reframes how we see others, and it changes the very way we engage with God.

I'd love to take credit for combining humor and the sacred, but I was beaten to it about thirty-five centuries ago. This is not a book about something new. This is a book about something we have lost. Honored by the ancients as a spiritual healing tool, celebrated by the great world religions, laughter is a deeply spiritual gift that we've lost somewhere along the way.

This book is written for all those who think that there must be more to the spiritual path than stale, rote dogma. It is dedicated to all those who yearn for a deeper sense of sacred intimacy and honesty. It is offered for all those who seek, all those who once sought but are now disillusioned, and all those who *thought* about seeking only to decide it wasn't worth the effort.

A word of warning: Do *not* read this book if you want to continue your spiritual journey via the same well-worn, rutted course. For those who prefer the status quo, beware; this is rebellious, even dangerous, material ahead. To leave known comfortable paths and head into new realms is unsettling, even scary. For some, introducing humor into the sacred can be like jarring bedrock. But beneath the bedrock lies undiscovered layers of rich, raw materials—natural resources that can transform our very lives.

We Are Hard-wired for Laughter

"An onion can make you cry, but there never was a vegetable invented to make people laugh."
—WILL ROGERS, COMEDIAN AND VAUDEVILLE PERFORMER

As with everything in life, there is always a "but."

"Oh, I love the idea of inviting humor onto the spiritual path,

... *but* I'm not funny."

... *but* I don't really have that great a sense of humor."

... *but* I'm really a pessimist at heart."

As adults, it is easy to see ourselves as pessimists or to believe that we have no sense of humor. Life can certainly beat the joy right out of us. But no matter how dormant our joy, the one thing life can't take is our innate ability to laugh. Laughter is a choice. In truth, human beings are hard-wired to laugh.

"Infants laugh almost from birth," says psychologist Steve Wilson in a WebMD feature on "Why We Laugh." "In fact, people who are born blind and deaf still laugh. So we know it's not a learned behavior. Humans are hard-wired for laughter."

Laughter is at the very core of creation. Ralph Waldo Emerson observed that "the earth laughs in flowers." Every morning the earth resonates with a joyful energy, whether through the rhythm of raindrops on a sidewalk in Brooklyn or the splash of a trout jumping in Tasmania. And every evening the same joyful singing is heard, from cricket songs on the South Carolina coast to the hissing and popping of the aurora borealis at the Arctic Circle. It is a joyful noise, the stuff of which we are made.

Many of us have been lulled into believing that humor is inappropriate in spiritual realms. Sometimes it's seen as disrespectful or even blasphemous. I can understand that. I was raised in a church where you would walk in, sit through the service, then walk out three inches shorter, bent over from all the guilt. Not exactly a wellspring of joy or laughter. Of course, the question we must ask is this: Inappropriate *according to whom?* (Hint: If this were multiple choice, God would not be included in the answer choices.)

I am not saying that laughter is the only face of God. However, if we are made in the image of the Divine, and if a core element of human beings is joy, then one face of the Holy surely must also be joy. Granted, it is one that is consistently ignored, but it is a core element nonetheless.

This book is not an attempt to teach people how to have a sense of humor or to train future stand-ups (although I do teach a class on stand-up comedy for clergy, brave soul that I am). Nor is it an attempt to put a glib spin on every event of our daily lives. I wrote this book for one simple reason: to remind us of our inherent ability to laugh.

Look, not everyone feels like being funny. You may not even feel happy. But somewhere deep down, your humanity yearns for joy and, if allowed, your heart will respond. Laughter is the gift that you received at birth, the one thing you were able to do freely when your age was in the single dig-its, the gift that may fade but never fully disappears. *Laugh Your Way to Grace* is intended to give you permission to recon-nect with your own sense of joy and hope—a deep life force that you were given at birth and still carry within.

Why "Grace"?

"I've learned that you can tell a lot about a person by the way he or she handles these three things: a rainy day, lost luggage, and tangled Christmas tree lights."

—MAYA ANGELOU, AMERICAN POET

I entitled this book *Laugh Your Way to Grace* for a number of reasons. Okay, yes, my middle name is Grace. So there's that. I also considered the quote by the great theologian Karl Barth, who said, "Laughter is the closest thing to the grace of God."

But I chose the word *grace* for a more personal reason. Unlike many Christian theologians, I don't fully resonate with the term *grace* from a salvation perspective. (My apologies to the two thousand years of Christian thought I've just ignored.) To me, "grace" feels truer when defined from a dance perspective.

Whether it's the Bolshoi Ballet, Appalachian cloggers, or an Aboriginal dance in the Northern Territory of Australia, choreographed movements of the human body are graceful. They are elegant, they are beautiful, and they share an intimate glimpse into the human spirit. And *that* is how I relate to the term *grace*. *Laugh Your Way to Grace* is about living life with elegance, beauty, and a generosity of spirit.

One caveat: Living gracefully during Shabbat dinner or Sunday service or meditation or prayer calls doesn't count. The spiritual path is not walked in the great halls of organized religion. At best, most of us spend an hour or so a week in formal worship or prayer. And let's face it: It's not hard to be pious for an hour.

The bulk of our spiritual life is trekked through the grit and reality of everyday life: preparing a report for work that bores you to tears, waiting in an "express" line at Walmart that is ten-people deep, making weekly grocery lists, vacuuming, mowing the lawn, stressing about your kids, worrying if you'll ever have enough money to retire. These are the stones of the spiritual path. These are the steps we trod day in and day out.

The ultimate question is how to introduce spiritual grace into this daily grind. As a veteran of the punch line and the pulpit, I believe that humor can empower us to live with elegance and beauty and a generosity of spirit. It is the one tool that can enable us to live our daily lives, our *spiritual* lives, with grace.

Where Are We Going with This?

"I think the most revolutionary act that you can commit in
our society today is to be happy."

—PATCH ADAMS, PHYSICIAN AND PROFESSIONAL CLOWN

This book is not "about" laughter. This is a book that demonstrates the power of laughter through the experience of laughter. While I try to offer points of learning, woven throughout are stories of my personal journey from law to comedy and ministry, including a two-year solo trip around the world. I hope you'll get a chuckle or two out of some of my tales.

Laugh Your Way to Grace is framed around two simple questions: Why we don't laugh, and what would happen if we did?

The book opens with "A Letter from God." Now this is something rarely heard: a humorous holy voice. I like to imagine God gently chiding us for losing this gift of laughter and offering us an intimate invitation to reclaim it.

The first section, "Why Aren't We Laughing?" reminds us of the forgotten humor legacy found in thousands of years of human spiritual history. It removes the harsh and fearful mask of a God who doesn't laugh, and exposes the world's attempts to convince us all that we do not deserve joy.

The second section, "What Would Happen If We Laughed?" explores the power of laughter to find perspective, to see past our differences, and to reclaim play in our everyday spiritual lives. It also addresses how laughter can empower us through hard times, bringing physical, emotional, and spiritual healing.

Each chapter ends with reflection questions that encourage you to take a more personal look at how the material may be integrated into your life.

In *The Book of Letters: A Mystical Alef-bait* (Jewish Lights), Rabbi Lawrence Kushner explores the sacred meaning and personalities of each letter of the Hebrew alphabet. For example, the second letter of the alphabet, *Bait,* looks like a box with the left side open. Rabbi Kushner explains, "You can walk into a *Bait* and you are at home. The Holy One wants us to be at home in His world. So the Torah begins with a *Bait* … 'In the beginning.'" I, too, believe that there is a sacred nature to language and the written word. The letter *L,* for example, the first letter of the word *laughter,* is also a symbol for the spiritual healing power of humor. The letter begins with a center point, then reaches out horizontally toward the world, and then up to the heavens.

It is my heartfelt wish that this book will bring this healing and wisdom to you, for laughter has the power to heal your heart, your relationship with others, and ultimately, your relationship with God.

I've studied theology and I've studied stand-up. And between the two, if I were looking for the presence of the Holy, I'd take stand-up any day. Stick with me on this; I am convinced that you can laugh your way to grace.

The Disciples sought to learn from the Master the stages he had passed through in his quest for the divine.

"God first led me by the hand," he said, "into the Land of Action, and there I dwelt for several years.

"Then He returned and led me to the Land of Sorrows; there I lived until my heart was purged of every inordinate attachment.

"That is when I found myself in the Land of Love, whose burning flames consumed whatever was left in me of self.

"This brought me to the Land of Silence, where the mysteries of life and death were bared before my wondering eyes."

"Was that the final stage of your quest?" they asked.

"No," the Master said. "One day God said, 'Today I shall take you to the innermost sanctuary of the Temple, to the very heart of God....'

"And I was led to the Land of Laughter."

—ANTHONY DE MELLO, *TAKING FLIGHT*

A Letter from God

Hello, my children,

I am so glad you picked up this book because we need to talk. Look, I appreciate all of your spiritual efforts: the custom meditation cushions, the Balinese incense, the PowerPoint liturgy. Really, I *do*. But something is wrong between us; something is missing. I sit with you and all your spiritual paraphernalia and feel, well ... empty. (I know that some of you do, too.) I listen to your prayers and think, where is the fire? Where's the intimacy? Then it dawned on me: We don't laugh together anymore.

Now *don't* roll your eyes at the Creator of the Universe. Humor is some powerful stuff. Have you forgotten that we share a sense of humor? Remember the whole "made in the image of the Divine" thing? And you know that you are the only creature that really laughs. (Well, there is that hyena that I made ... but let's not get sidetracked.) Besides, just consider the diversity of creation and then tell me that I don't have a sense of humor: heaven and earth, platypus and blowfish ... Jerry Springer and Jerry Falwell.

So what are you scared of? Where's your sense of humor? Did someone steal it? Did you lose it? Is it in the same place as those missing keys and umbrellas? I mean, come on! I gave you laughter as your first gift. A baby gift—don't you remember? Well, the sad truth is, unless you are under twelve years old or over seventy, you may *not*. It is no accident that laughter is honored most in the times of life you are closest to me: childhood, when you're fresh out of my arms, and then old age, when you're closing back in. (Ask any grandparent their thoughts on this.) It's those in-between years—those years you think you are the sole beneficiary of the universe—where you need this gift the most. So here's a little secret: You don't have to lose your sense of humor as you age (skin elasticity, maybe, but not humor).

Look, I'm not much into long-winded sermons, so I'll get to the point: I long for a more intimate relationship with you. And we can have it. It's not one bit different from how you develop intimacy in other relationships. You listen, you share, you build trust—and you laugh. They all relate. You can't laugh if you are not listening. And you can't authentically share if you hold part of yourself back as unlovable or unacceptable. You want healing? You have to give me all the pieces. I want *all* of you—the anger, the pain, the tears, *and* the laughter. I love it all. It's all holy.

Okay, so maybe you don't *have* to laugh to find me. But, I tell you what … come, sit with me in a quiet place. Tell me your stories. Share your dreams. Just laugh with me a bit. I'll take it from there.

—G.

Disclaimer

Being a trial lawyer for years, I would like to offer the following clarifications. While this may seem extreme, we must
always remember the words of Mark Twain: "The difference
in the right word and the almost right word is the difference
between lightening and lightening bug."

- When I say *God,* I mean God, Yahweh, Allah,
  Buddha, Jesus, Brahman, the Divine, the Creator, the
  Great Spirit, your Spirit, Mother Earth, the Universe,
  Big Bend National Park, key lime pie—however you
  encounter God.
- When I say *religion,* I mean all faith traditions, past
  and present. If you are searching or simply question-
  ing, that is a tradition.
- By *house of worship,* I mean the place where you find
  sacred time. This includes, but is not limited to,
  churches, synagogues, mosques, temples, meditation
  halls, monasteries, yoga classes, a mountain hike, or a
  couch with a Snuggy, a bowl of Lipton's French onion
  dip, and a bag of Ruffles.
- When I say *humor,* I am referring to joyful, therapeutic humor; humor that lifts us up. I am not speaking
  of scornful, hateful, or judgmental humor. Certainly
  humor can be misused. *So can sanctity*.

PART I

Why Aren't We Laughing?

"Laughter is day, and sobriety is night; a smile is the twi-
light that hovers gently between both, more bewitch-
ing than either."

—HENRY WARD BEECHER, NINETEENTH-CENTURY
CLERGYMAN AND REFORMER

1 Humor and Holiness Are *Not* Oxymorons
Finding My Way as an Ordained Comedian

God Is Not Funny

> "The man or woman who passes into the holy of holies and ceases to laugh is bringing into God's presence a mangled creature, one who is less than the full being that God intended him [or her] to be."
>
> —CONRAD HYERS, THEOLOGIAN

I grew up with a God who wasn't very funny. Then again, neither were Jesus nor the disciples or the prophets. From an early age, I knew God to be a stern combination of Walter Cronkite and Clint Eastwood in *High Plains Drifter*. Jesus had the same Cronkite-Eastwood personality, just contained in a body that had the obvious Aramaic features of a Nordic Viking.

Of course I grew up knowing other things about God. I knew God lived in heaven, in a gated community (with pearls) where all the saved Southern Baptists got houses based on the size of their church tithes. God put all the rest of the people (about 6.5 billion) in a place that resembled Phoenix in August.

I was also sure that God spoke in a Southern accent. I can't tell you how many times I have heard God say, "Be *stea-hul* and know I am-um *Gawd*."

This holy image, along with my love of fish sticks and a fear of spiders, is one of the many legacies I carried from my childhood. Actually, I dropped the gated community and Southern accent idea long ago. But the image of God as a somber, not so funny, even fearful character stuck for a long time. Need I explain what a huge problem this was for a comedian who felt called to the ministry?

Ministers (like God) were somber, teetotaling, big-haired versions of Gandalf in *The Lord of the Rings*. I, on the other hand, lacked hair height, liked Yellow Tail Shiraz, and most troubling, was a trial lawyer moonlighting as a stand-up comedian. (Oh, and I was a woman.) How could I be called to be a *minister*?

After a few years, I decided that maybe I should mention this "call" to a few friends, just to see if I was missing something. Their responses ranged from laughter combined with coughing fits to blank stares. "Who would call a comedian as their minister!" one cleric said, rolling his eyes. Others offered thoughts like, "You'll never get a job" or "The ministry requires *serious* theology." The doubters kept doubting, yet the call kept ringing.

You never know if a call is for you until you actually pick up the receiver and listen. To determine if this call was for me, I knew I needed to disengage, quiet the doubters, and explore this idea of ministry without the baggage of home. I also knew that travel, like humor, tends to shake things up and offer clarity. Three weeks later, I quit my job, put everything I owned in storage, packed a backpack, and left home for two years to figure things out. Of all the things I saw and did, one experience answered this question clearer than any other: working for Mother Teresa in Calcutta.

Laughter Is the GPS System for the Soul

> "Life is serious all the time, but living cannot be. You may have all the solemnity you wish in your neckties, but in anything important (such as sex, death, and religion), you must have mirth or you will have madness."
>
> —G. K. Chesterton, English writer and journalist

Twenty-one hours after boarding British Air in New York, I found myself standing at the doorway of Shishu Bhavan, Mother Teresa's orphanage. What I saw stopped me short: three and four children in one crib, tiny toddlers tied to bedposts, children crying out with no one to comfort them. After a moment, I gathered my courage and slowly stepped across the threshold.

That is when I encountered five-year-old Anna. Blind and deaf since birth, Anna could sense human presence from the vibrations of footsteps. As I walked by, she reached out and wrapped herself around my leg like a little koala bear. Not knowing what else to do, I sat down crossed-leg beside her. She immediately crawled into my lap and began rocking back and forth, laughing and singing. I quickly discovered that her favorite game was to hum a short tune and then press her ear up against me, feeling the vibrations as I hummed it back. She would laugh with joyous high-pitched squeals, hum a little tune back, and then press her ear against me again to feel the vibrations of my response. We played this game for hours.

In those moments of holding Anna, all questions about my call, about the connection between humor and the sacred, faded. Here in the laughter of this tiny girl was humor and the Holy made manifest. By Western standards, she had nothing: no home, no family, and barely enough food. Every day people came in and out of her life with no consistency and no promise of a home or permanence. Yet she greeted each with the same smile and tiny outstretched arms. For Anna, laughing was like breathing. It was her way of being in the world. She didn't offer her laughter to please. She didn't hope to get into heaven faster through her smile. She didn't know anything of "heaven." Anna laughed simply because she was alive.

I eventually left Calcutta, traveling for another two years through Asia, Africa, the Middle East, and ending with a drive to Alaska. What I found on this journey was example after example of "Anna" in different cultures and religious traditions.* After two years, twenty-three countries, and over thirty-one thousand miles, I knew my calling was to introduce humor (kicking and screaming, if need be) into the spiritual search.

My hunch ten years ago was right: Not only can a ministry of humor work, it is desperately needed. Good ministers, like comedians, stand in solidarity with their audience—not just through the silly, frustrating challenges in life, but in the places of greatest pain. Comedy says we are all in this together. It makes us feel a little less alone.

Laughter is the GPS system for the soul. Humor offers a revolutionary, yet simple, spiritual paradigm: If you can laugh at yourself, you can forgive yourself. And if you can forgive

---

*Which you will find detailed, free of charge, in chapter 2.

yourself, you can forgive others. Laughter heals. It grounds us in a place of hope.

Perhaps most important, laughter fosters intimacy and honesty in our relationships with each other and with God. In fact, laughter and faith are mutually dependent. Theologian Conrad Hyers explained, "Faith without laughter leads to dogma, and laughter without faith to despair." It is in these words that we begin to see a tiny glimmer of the power that can come from the merger of humor and the sacred.

It's All Holy

"Happiness is not a state to arrive at, but a manner of traveling."

—MARGARET LEE RUNBECK, AMERICAN AUTHOR

As a trained theologian, my favorite movie is, of course, *Kung Fu Panda*. The best part is when tortoise Zen master Oogway tries to convince Po that even though he's an overweight panda, his true destiny is to be a great dragon warrior. "Our destiny," he tells Po, "is usually found on the road we take to avoid it." And there, in one sentence, is my life as an ex-lawyer, turned stand-up comedian and minister.

My one regret? I wish I had realized earlier that my call was not a wrong number. In fact, that is why I wrote this book. Every person has a call, an invitation to bring all of who we are to the spiritual search. That includes the things that "don't fit the mold"—the tears, the anger, the joy, and the laughter. It's all holy.

We seem to have a much easier time sharing tears and remorse. We come slump-shouldered before God, proudly

bearing our shame, our fears, our self-denial, and our suffering. But, the part of our humanity that laughs is usually hidden away in shame.

Ironically, people speak of sacred tears. American author
Washington Irving wrote: "There is sacredness in tears.
They are not the mark of weakness, but of power. They
speak more eloquently than ten thousand tongues. They are
messengers of overwhelming grief ... and unspeakable love."
I believe that tears and laughter are almost indistinguishable.
Both can offer transformative experiences that cleanse, heal,
and restore our spirits. Yet, rarely do we give laughter that
chance.

But we bring laughter and humor into just about every
other aspect of life. Corporations use humor in workplace
training to address everything from presentation skills to
employee mental health. When the workday ends, sitcoms
and late-night comedians are invited into our living rooms to
calm and entertain us. When illness looms, modern medicine
hails humor as an alternative healing tool shown to stimulate
the immune system and increase wellness. Perhaps most
striking is that we usher humor into some of our most vulner-
able spaces, such as hospice and grief work. Yet, in our most
intimate place, our spiritual search, we tend to check our
humor at the doors of our houses of worship like we check
our coats.

These things that "don't fit the mold" are the very things
that give us life and spirit and our very humanity. Swiss psychologist Carl Jung called these the "shadow selves": the
parts of us that are alive and well, but that we would prefer
to keep on the "q.t." Here is the problem: We can't be made
whole if we don't offer up all the pieces. It doesn't matter
how wonderful God thinks we are, if we consider parts of

ourselves unworthy then we will forever find ourselves slump-shouldered, staring at the floor in holy realms.

Practice, Practice

"If at first you don't succeed, you're about average."

—MARION HAMILTON ALDERSON, EDITOR

This is an age of easy quick fixes:

"Drop ten pounds in a week!"
"Erase twenty years off your face in an hour!"
"Find your bliss today!"

We expect results immediately. We pray for three minutes, expecting to feel instantly grounded and pious. We do one downward dog in yoga, then look eagerly for our washboard abs. We chant *om* three times and consider ourselves fully enlightened beings.

Yet we don't hold the same expectations for other aspects of life. We hail the importance of practice in music, sports, art, and language. When the doctor prescribes a course of medication, we don't expect results after the first pill. When we bring home our new little Labrador Retriever puppy, we don't expect him to use the paper immediately. (We hope, but don't expect).

To develop anything of worth in life takes practice. That includes our spiritual path. And it most definitely includes laughter.

Yes, I said it: Laughter is a spiritual practice. You may not have heard it described this way, but practicing laughter is no different than practicing yoga or meditation or prayer. The transformative nature of any spiritual discipline comes with regular practice. When done consistently, it can eventually change our lives. If we make time to invite joy into our lives each day, we will become more aware of joy and laughter in our lives and in the world. Eventually, laughter will become an innate part of who we are.

Practicing something is a bit like doing housework. Personally, I hate doing windows. In New York City there is no motivation to do windows because in thirty minutes they will be clouded right back over with dirt and smog. But I have to do them because if I don't, even on the clearest, sunniest day, the light in my house will be dimmer. And if I look through that dirty window long enough (which, believe me, I have), I begin to think that the world itself has become hazed in that same shade of light brown.

It's the same in our lives. We all live with patterns that drive what we do and how we perceive things, patterns that are simply years of emotional dirt and smog. The danger of these patterns is that they can affect our viewpoint; they can dim the light in our houses. And worse, over time, we forget how things used to be.

Making laughter and joy a consistent part of our daily routine is like doing windows. It cleans away old patterns that block our vision. It allows more light into our otherwise dimly lit houses. Henry David Thoreau wrote, "Though we travel the world over to find the beautiful, we must carry it with us or we find it not." Laughter is the beauty and the light and the spirit we all carry within. We just need to acknowledge and welcome it as a gift from and a means to the Holy.

REFLECTIONS

Did you grow up in organized religion? If so, describe the minister, priest, or rabbi you grew up with. If not, what was your impression of clergy? Did they laugh? Smile? Were they warm people or arms-length people? How did this influence your image of God?

Laughter, in a way, is about forgiveness. Think of a time when you were able to laugh at your shortcomings rather than judge yourself. How did that change how you felt about yourself? Did giving yourself a break offer a heightened sense of forgiveness for others?

Recall a time you were in a comedy club or watching comedy on television with others. When you laughed together at the same jokes, how did you feel? Did you feel a sense of solidarity? Less alone?

Think about Conrad Hyers's statement: "Faith without laughter leads to dogma, and laughter without faith to despair." Do you think this is it true? Why or why not? What experiences in your life do those words remind you of?

2 The Lost Branch of the Family Tree

Remembering Our Legacy of Laughter

The Pete Townshend Question

"You gotta be careful if you don't know where you're going, because you might not get there."

—YOGI BERRA, MAJOR LEAGUE BASEBALL PLAYER

One of my many favorite memories as a minister is the Sunday I began the sermon by having the choir sing "Who Are You?" by Pete Townshend of The Who. Swaying in their eggplant-colored robes, the classically trained sextet belted out, *"Whoooo are you? Who Who Who Who?"*

Granted, this song is not high on the list of great liturgical preludes, but it certainly beats music about fountains of blood and baby lambs. I used it because it was joyful and fun. I also used it because this song invited my congregation into one of life's great questions: "Who are you?"

As human beings we rarely ask ourselves this question. Yet without this insight, we lose touch with who we are. We lose our legacy. It's like the theologian John Kenny said, "If you don't know who you are, you act like who you ain't."

One of the great lost spiritual legacies is laughter. For thousands of years humor and laughter have played an essential role in our human search for enlightenment and spiritual connection. Unfortunately, we seem to have lost track of that branch of the family tree. It's high time we listened to Pete, did a little genealogy, and asked *Whooooo are you? Who Who Who Who?*"

Why Is Everyone Else Laughing?

> "Why waste your time looking up your family tree? Just
> go into politics, and your opponents will do it for you."
> —MARK TWAIN

Recently, my step-daughter went on genealogy.com and constructed my family tree. I was so excited, as I had always fancied myself a Scottish princess with bloodlines tracing back to Robert the Bruce. In the end, however, it became apparent that I was nothing but a European mutt. Worse, the only historical figures to whom I was related were Elvis Presley, and Bonnie and Clyde. I guess for self-awareness, if nothing else, the clarification was important. At least now when I have the urge to put on a sequined jumpsuit and rob a Citibank, I'll know why.

Earlier in my life, I had done research on a family tree of a different kind. As a comedian called to the ministry, I desperately wanted to find family—people who had a similar perspective on laughter and the Holy. I looked far and wide, yet for many years found no such kin.

It's kind of like the story of the ugly duckling. There, a little bird hatches in a barnyard, yet doesn't seem to be like any of his brothers and sisters. He ends up traveling place to place, trying to find home. Finally, as he is swimming in a pond, he sees a group of graceful swans. When he looks in the water, he is surprised to discover that in fact he, too, is a swan. He had found his true family and lived happily ever after.

Sometimes, to find true family you have to go way out on the limbs of the family tree. Since my familiar Western religious traditions weren't showing much promise, I decided to venture out onto those outer branches to see for myself what the rest of the world thought. Thus began my two-year solo trip around the world, which included my stint with Mother Teresa's mission and all points beyond.

Enlightenment through a Smile

"There are many things that even the wise fail to do, while the fool hits the point.
Unexpectedly discovering the way to life in the midst of death, he bursts out in hearty laughter."

—SENGAI, ZEN MASTER

One of my first ventures on the trip was a trek through Nepal, monastery to monastery. I prepared for it as best I knew how, packing several Thich Nhat Hanh books and a small, purse-sized Zen garden, complete with its own tiny rake.

Unfortunately, I didn't have time to rake. I was busy praying not to die on the Russian transport helicopter that flew us from Kathmandu to Lukla, our first stop. Luckily, the prayers worked, and we landed on a tiny grass airstrip high in the Himalayas. After lunch and several hours of hard uphill climbing (beginning at ten thousand feet), we approached our first monastery. As we walked up, its door swung abruptly open and a monk with a huge smile on his face greeted us.

"Americans?" he shouted.

"Yes," we responded.

"Oh!" he said. "Stock market crashed today! Big crash! Very bad. So sorry." Then he started laughing.

Given that most of my nest egg from my old law days was sitting in the market, I wasn't laughing.

Still cackling, he invited us in and led us to our rooms. After settling in, we sat down to an early dinner with the monks, including my friend who had gleefully greeted us at the door.

Still smarting from the stock market announcement, I turned to him and asked, "Why did you greet us with a message of the stock market crash and then laugh hysterically?"

"Because it's funny," he said, laughing again. "People worry so much about accumulating money. Yet it never brings them what they truly want." He smiled and went back to eating his *dal bhat*.

Later that evening, I went to the monastery's library. As I scanned the shelves, a title caught my eye: *The Laughing Buddha: Zen and the Comic Spirit* by Conrad Hyers. Within minutes I was lost in the book.

I quickly learned that my laughing monk friend was not alone in his perspective. In fact, his sharp sense of humor was a trait he shared with most Buddhist followers, especially those in the Zen tradition.

There is a well-known Zen story where one of the Buddha's disciples revealed his enlightenment through a wordless smile. The smile was transmitted by a succession of twenty-eight Indian patriarchs until the Bodhidharma brought it to China, where the smile transformed into thundering laughter.

One of the most famous Zen figures is that of Hotei, a big-bellied, eccentric monk who is said to have wandered through the land during the tenth century with a cloth bag over his shoulder. According to legend, he never spoke, but only giggled and cackled. Refusing monastic life, his religious life consisted simply of playing with the village children, since only children and fools knew what priests and monks did not.

At breakfast the next morning, I told my laughing friend about the book. He smiled and nodded.

"More bad news in the market today," he said, smiling. This time, I was the one who laughed.

My Kind of God

"Krishna burst into loud laughter and as he laughed his body seemed to become a roaring fire with throngs of gods flaring from it like flashes of lightning."
—*MAHABHARATA*, SANSKRIT EPIC POEM

A month later, I flew from Kathmandu to New Delhi. As I emerged from the Air India flight and took my first look at Delhi, I knew there'd been a mistake. It was clear that I had accidentally boarded not Air India, but the space shuttle for an unknown, but gorgeous, new galaxy. The images, the smells, the gods—all so different from my limited Western experience.

In my home galaxy, God had one face (Jesus), and Jesus had one expression (a frown). Didn't matter where he was or what he was doing, he was frowning.

Healing a leper: frowning.

Holding a baby lamb: frowning.

Drinking wine: frowning.

You can imagine my surprise when I learned that in this new galaxy, the Hindu tradition honored a god with more than one face, and some of those faces were smiling.

After deplaning, I hailed a rickshaw to my hostel. As I rode along, I noticed smiling elephant heads over many of the doorways of the shops and buildings.

"What is the deal with the elephant heads?" I asked my driver.

With a look of disbelief, my driver shook his head and responded, "It is—of course—Ganesha."

The most beloved and popular of all Hindu gods, he explained, Ganesha is a smiling elephant deity with a huge pot belly, which legend says came from gobbling too much candy.

Now this was *my* kind of god.

Born from the laughter of the deity Shiva, Ganesha is the god of new beginnings. His image is found over doorways throughout India, guarding the entrance from harm and blessing those who step through new thresholds.

"You mean the Hindu people think God actually smiles?" I asked, shocked.

He looked at me with amusement. In a moment he stopped in front of a Hindu temple and pointed to a statue toward the top. It was a little, blue, fat smiling baby dancing on the head of a cobra.

"This is God as a baby—baby Krishna. He laughs all the time," my driver said. As the story goes, when Krishna was born, a brilliant light and sense of cheerfulness fell upon his parents, and he shone upon them with a beautiful smile. The baby Krishna celebrates new consciousness, playfulness, and joy.

Looking at the portico, I wondered if Ganesha or Krishna would want to hang out with the Jesus with whom I'd grown up. I looked again at the cute, blue baby with the mischievous smile. No, I didn't think so. And you know what? I wouldn't blame them.

Laughing in the Ear of God

"[The] Lord will rejoice over you in great gladness;
he will renew you with his love; he will exult over
you with loud singing as on a day of festival."
—ZEPHANIAH 3:17–18

I left India and continued on to Israel and Jerusalem. On my first day in Jerusalem, I decided to walk the main thoroughfare, Ben Yehuda Street. I stopped for a cup of coffee. As I sat down at the outdoor café table, I spied him. I squinted and tried to focus harder. But, no, there he was, dancing down Ben Yehuda—a man dressed in an orange wig, with red overall shorts and red striped socks. I stared at him in disbelief. Then I began to look around at the rest of the crowd. On the shoulders of a man not far from me was a little girl dressed in a rabbit outfit; not far from the rabbit was a woman on stilts; and at the far end of the street was a cowboy with a ten-gallon hat and chaps.

Was it jetlag? Was it too much malaria medication when I was in India? Did I need a new glasses prescription? No. I had simply arrived in Jerusalem at Purim.

Commemorating the deliverance of the Jewish People from the Persian leader Haman as set forth in the book of Esther, Purim is a raucous celebration filled with revelry, carnival, and festivities. It is observed each year on the fourteenth of the Jewish month of Adar, in keeping with the date Haman had marked for their death.

Throughout Jerusalem and all over Israel, Purim is celebrated with parades, games, dances, and festivals. People eat pastries filled with poppy seeds called "Haman's ears." As the book of Esther is read in the synagogues, children shake noisemakers to drown out the name "Haman." And of course, Ben Yehuda is packed with clowns and rabbits and cowboys.

Some people even wear their costumes to the Wailing Wall. As the remains of the ancient western wall of the great Temple, the Wailing Wall is the most sacred of places; a place where one has the "ear of G-d."*

I later learned that humor has long been a tool of healing and survival of the Jewish People. The Talmud, a central sacred text of Judaism, speaks of a God who laughs. Holocaust survivors, including well-known Jewish authors Elie Wiesel and Viktor Frankl, have written about how imprisoned Jews used humor for empowerment and emotional survival. During the Nazi occupation of Romania, for example, the author Emil Dorian composed this short prayer: "Dear God, for five thousand years we have been your chosen people. Enough! Choose another one now."

After hearing that, I then understood why the Jewish People make up approximately 3 percent of the population

---

*"G-d" is a way of noting the name of the Divine in the traditional Jewish faith. Based on Deuteronomy 12:3, it is done out of respect to avoid any possibility of defacing or destroying the name of God.

of the United States yet 90 percent of American stand-up comedians.

That day on Ben Yehuda brought me a whole new understanding of humor in religious realms. Laughing in the ear of God? I might well have to convert.

Sacred Clowns

> "The Creator made humans able to walk and talk, to see and hear … to do everything. But the Creator wasn't satisfied. Finally, the Creator made humans laugh, and when they laughed and laughed, the Creator said, 'Now you are fit to live.'"
>
> —TRADITIONAL APACHE STORY

After one year, seven jumbo packages of Imodium, three retreads on my hiking boots, and eighty rolls of film, I returned home … only to decide I wasn't ready to settle down. So I simply transferred my backpack from British Air to the back of my Jeep Wrangler and drove from JFK International Airport in New York City to Alaska.

For the first few days, I didn't stop much. (I always found anything east of the Mississippi pretty boring.) It was only when I passed through the plains of Kansas, over the Rockies, and into the desert Southwest that I began to slow down.

One bright sunny afternoon, I found myself on the Navajo reservation in northwest Arizona. Pulling into a local gas station, I noticed a poster over the pump announcing a tribal dance.

Three hours later, I was sitting in a field watching the performance. I was surprised how quickly I was drawn into the chants and movement. Deeply spiritual, the dance felt more like worship than anything I had experienced back East.

Powerful as it was, however, the ceremony itself was not what I remembered years later. What I remembered were the sacred clowns.

Right in the middle of what seemed a very sacred moment, a dancer dressed in ragged clothes appeared and began to mimic the other dancers, who were dressed as various deities.

As the crowd laughed and clapped, the clowns continued to make fun of the other dancers and members of the crowd. I turned to a local man standing next to me and asked about the clowns. He shook his head and smiled.

"It's complicated," he said. "The clowns can say and do things that others cannot. Sometimes they come to teach lessons. Other times they remind us what is important or simply bring a moment of release."

I thought about what a heyday these clowns would have in some of our houses of worship: mimicking the self-important clergy, making the congregation laugh in places of pain, reminding us that we were there to worship rather than argue about the color of the altar flowers. I sighed to myself. If only …

> "If there is no joy and freedom, it is not a church: it is simply a crowd of melancholy people basking in a religious neurosis."
>
> —STEVE BROWN, AUTHOR AND SEMINARY PROFESSOR

The trip continued like this for two full years. With every twist and turn, I found examples of people who honored humor and the sacred. Finally, I had found a clear answer to the question, *"Who are you?"* We are a people who, for thousands of years, have seen joy in creation, have honored humor as a means to enlightenment, and have believed in a God, a life force, who laughs. We are a family with a powerful legacy of humor. We just need to be reminded every once in a while.

REFLECTIONS

Can you imagine God smiling? How does a smiling image of God fit, or not fit, with what you have been taught about God?

How might it feel to laugh in the ear of God? Does this sound blasphemous? According to whom? What thought or image would you need to revise in order to enjoy a bit of the Creator's humor?

How might your prayer or worship change if a sacred clown were present? If you actually laughed with God?

3 Spiritual Geliophobia

The Fear of Laughing in the Presence of God

The Legend of Mad Dog Murphy

> "We cannot really love anybody with whom we never laugh."
>
> —AGNES REPPLIER, AMERICAN ESSAYIST

Once upon a time, there was a big, scary law school professor named Mad Dog Murphy. He lived in the stacks of the Wake Forest University library, eating unsuspecting first-year students for his mid-morning snack. Or so we all believed.

Passed down from generation to generation, the stories of Mad Dog had become part of the very fabric of the first-year law school experience.

"I had him twenty years ago, and he wadded up one of my exam answers in front of the class and ate it!" quipped a young professor.

"That's nothing," said an upper classman. "This one guy in our class showed up unprepared, and Mad Dog called him to the front, handed him a piece of paper, and said, 'Here's the phone number for Taco Bell; go get yourself a job you can handle.'"

At 9 a.m. on my first day of a course on civil procedure, the door cracked open and in walked this lumbering, white-haired giant. He laid his books on the podium and peered out at our class with a detached stare.

"I am sure you have heard all kinds of stories about me," he said, his grin growing. "And, I must admit … they are all true."

No one laughed.

No one smiled.

No one was even *breathing*.

He looked around the room, as if expecting a response. Getting none, he sighed, put on his bifocals, and looked down the role. It was like waiting for the executioner's call. And sure enough, my time on earth had ended.

"Ms. Sparks!"

I gulped and tried to stand up—a difficult task since I had lost all feeling in my legs.

"Please tell us what you know of subject matter jurisdiction."

I had read the assignment fifty times, memorizing every word. Yet as I stared at the book, I couldn't manage a sound.

"Ms. Sparks?"

Silence.

"Not to be rude, but how long do you think it might be before we are graced with your answer?"

Silence.

"Well, perhaps the class would like to hear a joke while you are thinking."

I looked up in disbelief.

"Does anyone know the difference between a dead snake in the road and a dead lawyer in the road?"

No one said a word.

"The snake has skid marks in front of it."

Of course there was silence. No one dared laugh, in fear of drawing attention to themselves.

Looking around at the shell-shocked class, he said, "Ms. Sparks, I believe what we have here is a clear-cut case of geliophobia. Perhaps for extra credit you can define geliophobia?"

Unable to articulate even a one-syllable "no," I simply shook my head.

"It means," he said with a disappointed sigh, "the fear of laughing."

Mad Dog Returns

"From our sour-faced saints, good Lord, deliver us."

—TERESA OF ÁVILA, SIXTEENTH-CENTURY MYSTIC

Ten years after graduating from law school, I found myself back in a university lecture hall, having traded my civil procedure textbook for a Bible. It wasn't that big of a jump, law school to seminary. Same skills, different boss.

There was one similarity for which I was not prepared. In the hallowed halls of Union Seminary, I was about to encounter another Mad Dog. And this time it wasn't a professor.

An early hint came while giving my first sermon. Of course, as a comedian, I couldn't resist starting with something funny.

"It is a dangerous thing, giving a sermon without humor," I began. "Just ask the Apostle Paul. *'And upon the first day of the week, when the disciples came together to break bread, Paul*

preached unto them ... and continued his speech until midnight.
And there sat in a window a certain young man named Eutychus,
being fallen into a deep sleep: and as Paul was long preaching, he
sunk down with sleep, and fell down from the third loft, and was
taken up dead' (Acts 20:7–9, KJV)."

Okay. So it wasn't worthy of Caroline's Comedy Club in
New York. But, for a pulpit, it wasn't bad.

I looked around at the congregation expectantly.

Nothing.

Not a snicker.

Not a smile.

I was stunned. I knew many of these folks. They were
funny people who were quick to laugh.

"Let me say this again: taken up *dead?*"

Silence.

"He fell out the window because the Apostle Paul talked
too much and was boring!"

Silence.

"Oh, come on ya'll, that is *funny.*"

A few stern faces nodded in agreement.

Stunned, I continued with the sermon, consciously cutting
any remaining funny passages as I went.

After the service, I asked one of my friends what
happened.

"Was the opening that bad?"

"No," she said with a big smile. "It was great. Really
funny. Why?"

"Well, if something is funny, usually people laugh." I
paused, looking at her with a help-me-out-here expression.

"Well yeah ... but this is church. It's different."

All of a sudden I heard Mad Dog's words ringing
through: "Geliophobia, Ms. Sparks, is the fear of laughter."

If there were such a thing as geliophobia, then there must be spiritual geliophobia: the fear of laughing in the presence of God.

In law school, we were scared to laugh in Mad Dog's presence because of what we had been told about him. In worship, people were scared to laugh based on what they had been told about God. The longer I preached, the more people I encountered who seemed to have grown up with the same legend of a big, scary deity whose presence invited fear more than joy. As a minister, I had become a PR rep for Mad Dog God.

The Legend of Mad Dog God

"God has never spoken to me directly, but I have heard him clear his throat."

— MEISTER ECKHART, MEDIEVAL CHRISTIAN MYSTIC

Once upon a time, there was a big, scary deity named Mad Dog God. He lived tucked away in a far-off place, striking people with plagues and lightning bolts for his mid-morning entertainment. Or so most of us believed.

Passed down from generation to generation, the stories of Mad Dog God had become part of the very fabric of our religious experience.

Every Sunday we'd hear the stories:

Then the earth reeled and rocked; the foundations of the heavens trembled and quaked, because God was angry. Smoke went up from his nostrils, and devouring fire from his mouth; glowing coals flamed forth from him. (2 Samuel 22:8–9)

> The LORD shall smite thee with consumption, and with a fever, and with an inflammation, and with an extreme burning, and with the sword, and with blasting, and with mildew; and they shall pursue thee until thou perish. (Deuteronomy 28:22, KJV)

> O God, break the teeth in their mouths.... Let them be like the snail which dissolves into slime ... consume them in wrath, consume them till they are no more. (Psalm 58:6, 8; 59:13)

Unfortunately, God hasn't helped by offering any clarifying information. The best we get is when Moses asks God's name in Exodus, and God says, "I am, that I am" (3:14). The ancient Hebrew translation works out to something like, "What you see is what you get."

In the church I attended as a child, this scary God stared back at me from the stained-glass windows surrounding our pew. On the right side, near the front, was a depiction of God drowning Pharaoh's army in the Red Sea. On the left side was a very unhappy Jesus hanging on a cross. The window in the back had God destroying the world with a flood. And the window closest to us had an image of God that looked like my Uncle Claude D., the only person I ever knew who scowled while he slept.

This was not a God you wanted to annoy. Nor was it a God from whom you wanted to draw attention. Conversation with this God was (a) avoided at all costs, or (b) done so through closed eyes and silence, or stale rote prayers, so as not to raise any undo holy attention.

As a child, I had no way of knowing that this legend of Mad Dog God had been created by someone other than God. I didn't realize that there actually might be a God behind the legend ... didn't realize, that is, until the Sunday of the hemorrhoid story.

And God Smote Them with Hemorrhoids

"God is a comedian playing to an audience who is afraid
  to laugh."

—VOLTAIRE, FRENCH PHILOSOPHER

It was a hot August Sunday, and the ladies of the church were fanning as fast as their stretch polyester dress sleeves would allow. The minister rose and walked to the pulpit to read the scripture for the day.

"Today's scripture, 1 Samuel, chapter five, verses 1–12, tells us what God does to his enemies."

I settled in with my fan and crayons, knowing I had a good hour or more to sit still and be quiet.

"'*And it was* so,'" the pastor's voiced boomed, "'*that, after the Philistines had carried the Ark of the Covenant about, the hand of the LORD was against the city with a very great destruction: and he smote the men of the city, both small and great, and they had 'emerods' in their secret parts.'*'"

The fans stopped.

Eyes darted about.

Notwithstanding the sneaky King James language of "emerods,"* we all knew what was meant. I had heard about hemorrhoids from the whisperings of my older relatives. While I wasn't sure what they were, I knew it had something

---

*Because I know you are *dying* to know—the etymology in Webster's for the term *hemorrhoid* is from the Middle English *emeroides,* plural, and from the Anglo-French *emorroides*.

to do with the bathroom, which, of course, is top on the list of a seven-year-old's humor.

I immediately put my hand over my mouth, but it was too late. My laugh pierced the holy silence.

"Susan Grace!" I heard my mother whisper, as she placed a firm hand on my arm.

"But... *hemorrhoids*?" I said with my hand still over mouth.

She glared at me and whispered, "Don't you laugh in this service. It's rude, and Jesus doesn't like it."

I learned two conflicting lessons that day: (1) people never, *ever* laughed in church, and (2) they worshipped a God who used hemorrhoids to punish people. That's when I knew that there had to be a God behind the legend. Not unlike Mad Dog Murphy.

The Man Behind the Legend

"I must first give up the notion that I know what I am looking at... for the shadows cast by a tree on the ground may hold more possibility than the tree itself."

—BARBARA BROWN TAYLOR, AUTHOR AND EPISCOPAL PRIEST

In December of my second year of law school, I was picked for the International Moot Court Team. That was the good news. The bad news? The faculty advisor was Mad Dog.

"Come in, Ms. Sparks!" he bellowed from his desk as I walked in for our first meeting. "Welcome! I'm glad to have you on the team."

Once again I felt my throat close up.

"Thank you," I barely managed. Not wanting to make eye contact, I began looking around at various things in his office. On his desk was a photo of him on a boat, smiling and laughing with his family. Taped on his wall were various *Far Side* cartoons. And sitting on top of his civil procedure text-book was a small, stuffed Rottweiler with cotton coming out of its mouth.

"You have a stuffed Mad Dog on your desk?" I blurted, before I caught myself.

"It was a gift from one of your classmates," he said smugly.

I stared at him in disbelief.

He smiled, knocking his pipe on the bottom of his shoe. "Is the story about me eating an exam still floating about? It's one of my personal favorites."

I stared at him. "You mean ... ?"

"Ms. Sparks, you've been listening to too many third-years. Here you are studying to be a trial lawyer, and yet you break one of the cardinal rules of evidence—listening to hearsay."

I thought about it for a minute. Sure he was tough, and sure he expected a lot, but in reality, Mad Dog had never done anything that even remotely resembled the monster about whom we'd all heard.

Perhaps he was right. Perhaps we had been pre-programmed to experience him as a fearful, intimidating presence. Perhaps we had created an image of this man that was, at a minimum, limited or, at worst, totally wrong.

"Well ... your snake joke our first day *was* pretty funny," I said slowly, finally making eye contact.

"Glad you liked it! There's plenty more where that came from," he said, chuckling. And with that, our relationship began to change.

As I finally began to let down around Mad Dog, I found a great resource and a friend. He helped me get a job after law school. He listened to my stories as a first-year associate. Ultimately, he wrote me a recommendation for seminary.

When fear changes to respect, we begin to see people in a very different way. We start to ask questions, we share, we ask for help. We also begin to laugh more because we feel safe.

Ironically, over the years I found Mad Dog to be a warm, joyful person, someone with whom I've shared many a story and many a laugh. His nickname now makes me smile. I just had to see the man behind the legend.

The God Behind the Legend

"In hell there is no hope and no laughter.
In purgatory there is no laughter, but there is hope.
In heaven, hope is no longer necessary because laughter reigns."

—DANTE, ITALIAN POET

In much the same way as I had been predisposed to dread Mad Dog Murphy, I had been pre-programmed to experience Mad Dog God as a fearful, intimidating presence. Early on, I had formed an image of God that was, at a minimum, limited or, at worst, totally wrong.

It is easy to do. None of us was born with a microchip providing us with "the" image of God. Rather, from birth on, we tend to gather information from our religious upbringing, our families, our cultures to construct our personal image of God. In fact, the great psychoanalyst Sigmund Freud spent his lifework in effect reversing the Genesis process, arguing that it is human beings who create God in their own image.

In truth, we sometimes like having a Mad Dog God around: an angry, smoking-nosed, striking-people-into-slime kind of God; a God who will ensure that right will triumph and evil-doers will be punished. We fear that a buddy God, a God who laughs, is not going to protect us or make the world safe from harm. A laughing God is not what we yearn for when the chips are down.

We have to look past that fear and those stale images. Power and laughter are hardly mutually exclusive. God is big enough to wield both.

As with Mad Dog Murphy, it was only when I began to look around God's "office" that I began to see the God behind the legend. There were God's family photos in the faces of the wondrous diversity of humanity; there were God's cartoons in the great ironies of everyday life; and of course, there was God's sense of humor reflected in the laughter of little children and the playfulness of newborn creatures. And with that realization, my relationship with God began to change.

> "Forgive, O Lord, my little jokes on Thee and I'll forgive
>   Thy great big one on me."
>
> —ROBERT FROST, AMERICAN POET

What if we changed our relationship and approached God as a respected friend, not a fearful authoritarian figure? What if we felt safe enough to believe that God is strong *and* funny?

There is a big difference when we approach God with respect rather than fear. We open up, ask questions, seek opinions.

As we begin to trust, we share stories.

Eventually, we laugh.

It's time to end our spiritual geliophobia. It's time to unpack our fears and find the God behind the legend. Encountering the Holy might just take on an entirely new meaning. Just try it. You may be surprised.

REFLECTIONS

What images of God do you remember from childhood?

How did your parents act around God? In worship? In prayer? Was God treated like a fearful authoritarian figure or a close friend?

How do you image God now? Has it changed?

If you treated God like you do your best friend, how might your relationship with God change?

4 Eating Dessert on the Titanic
The Opportunity for Joy Is Now

You Can't Laugh Until ...

> "PURITANISM: the haunting fear that somewhere, somehow, someone ... is happy."
>
> —H. L. Mencken, U.S. editor

My mom made Rice Krispies Treats that were better than anyone else's in our neighborhood. They were the perfect combination of flavors: gooey marshmallows, lots of butter, Rice Krispies cereal, and a secret ingredient, which I later learned to be Jif peanut butter (smooth). No one could match them.

As with all things, though, there was a catch. We were not allowed a Rice Krispies bar without finishing dinner first. In order to get within reach of this crunchy heaven, piles of brussels sprouts, okra, stewed tomatoes, and broccoli had to be plowed through. Some nights (usually the ones with stewed tomatoes and okra), I just couldn't do it. And if I didn't finish dinner, I didn't get a bar.

I never understood why we couldn't eat the bar at the same time as the stewed tomatoes. It sure would have made them go down easier. But, alas, that was not part of our Puritan work-ethic diet.

Thanks to this regime, I, like millions of others, grew up believing dessert always comes after dinner and never before. And like the marshmallow creme in those bars, that lesson oozed into every aspect of life.

> You can't eat dessert until you finish dinner.
> You can't go out and play until you finish practicing piano.
> You can't take vacation until you've cleaned out your in box.
> You can't retire until you have the magical dollar amount X squirreled away in your bank account.
> You can't feel good about yourself until you've lost those last ten pounds.
> You can't laugh until you've wallowed in every hard, depressing, stressful, harsh thing—first. (It's no wonder desserts is stressed spelled backward.)

While this may be a good lesson at age seven, it poses a major problem at age forty. Newspaper columnist Erma Bombeck best identified the problem with this observation: "Think about the tragic nature of the women on the Titanic who, on that fateful evening, said no to dessert."

Notwithstanding the uncertain and precarious nature of life, we continually say "no" to life's joys and desserts. And for what? Another check on the "to-do" list? An extra line on the résumé? The sad thing is the extra check or résumé entry doesn't guarantee us anything. Certainly not happiness. As Erma suggested, we never know when the ship of life will sail us smoothly home or slam us into an iceberg. Best to order dessert now.

We've Been Plutoed!

"Be yourself. Everyone else is taken."
    —OSCAR WILDE, LATE-NINETEENTH-CENTURY PLAYWRIGHT

Every year, the American Dialect Society picks a "word of the year." Past winners include "governator" in 2003, inspired by Governor Arnold Schwarzenegger and his role in the movie *Terminator,* and "truthiness" in 2005, a word created by Stephen Colbert to describe facts one wishes to be true. My all-time favorite was the winner from 2006.

That year the International Astronomical Union (IAU) decided that, based on its less-than-acceptable size and orbit shape, Pluto would be downgraded from a planet to a dwarf planet. Thus was born the term *plutoed,* meaning "devalued."

I felt for Pluto. I really did. Seventy-six years of being a happy little planet... then almost overnight, it's *nothing*. And all because a few individuals decided to tweak the definition of what was necessary to succeed as a planet.

Blogs demanding reinstatement and angry op-ed pleas ensued. But to no avail. Pluto was out. The global outcry was not surprising.

Being plutoed is certainly not limited to planets. Almost daily, the world tweaks the definition of what is necessary to "succeed." One moment you are gainfully employed, and the next, the job title is "redefined" and you are out. *Plutoed!*

One day you are in a happy relationship, and the next, your partner or spouse has determined that he or she needs something different to be happy. Different, that is, from you. *Plutoed!*

One day you are happily making mac-and-cheese in your perfectly acceptable size 12 chinos, and the next, you are told if you aren't a size 0 or less, you aren't loveable. *Plutoed!*

Like the sad little planet, we have allowed ourselves to be plutoed by what the world says we are worth. Downgraded. Demoted. Devalued.

Is it any wonder we continually say "no" to life's joys and desserts? It's hard to feel joy when we are told we aren't enough. It's hard to be happy when the world says we are not worthy. It's hard to laugh when we are told we aren't loveable.

> "Laughter is the sun that drives winter from the human face."
>
> —VICTOR HUGO, FRENCH POET, PLAYWRIGHT

It's not like we get any help from heavenly realms—at least according to many of God's PR folks. According to them, because of a one-time picnic incident with an apple, human beings are "something to be fixed," relegated to a life of judgment and shame rather than joy and hope. Anything human, anything bodily, is to be controlled or suppressed—especially laughter. Saint Augustine warned "human beings laugh and weep, and it is a matter for weeping that they laugh."

And sadly, we believe it. Wordy John Calvin, one of God's more noisy public relations guys, offered this unfortunate prayer: "Surely, O Lord... we know that for the justest causes thy wrath is kindled against us... [and] though thou mightest take much severer punishment upon us than before, and thus inflict blows an hundredfold more numerous... we confess that we are worthy of them."

Plutoed.

We buy into what the world says we are capable of and end up suffering a sort of emotional osteoporosis. Bent over under the weight of shame, our eyes fall from the horizon to the floor. And, unfortunately, that's a weight we have a hard time letting go of.

Human Lowriders

"Most people are about as happy as they make up their minds to be."

—ABRAHAM LINCOLN

My dad, Herb, was a man who believed in being overly prepared, especially when it came to cars. He was actually one of the first in our neighborhood to sport a "lowrider"—not because the suspension had been modified (like most classic lowriders), but because of the inordinate amount of roadside assistance items he carried in the trunk. Tucked neatly away in the cavernous trunk of his 1964 baby blue Buick LaSabre were three golf umbrellas, two Totes rain hats, several sets of emergency flashers, a road atlas from 1952, three tool boxes, an "extra" spare tire, and, of course, chains and an aluminum space blanket. (These were in case he encountered a blizzard in the .3 mile drive from our home to his office—his office in Charlotte, North Carolina).*

Most of us tend to be on the Herb side, carrying around things we don't really need, weighting ourselves down with unnecessary baggage, going through life like human "lowriders."

---

*In all fairness, there was the blizzard of 1948 in which Herb was the only human being in the state of North Carolina who made it to work.

We would much prefer to let negative comments Velcro them-selves directly to our psyche, rather than use the Teflon approach and let them slip immediately off and away.

Unfortunately, as we carry this negative baggage along, it begins to sink in. And before we know it, we start to believe it. We begin to think we can't do anything right, beating our-selves up for every mistake we make.

> "A person who doesn't make mistakes, doesn't make anything."
>
> —WILLIAM CONNOR MAGEE,
> NINETEENTH-CENTURY IRISH CLERGYMAN

My grandmother, Emma Sue, had a garden at her farm in the North Carolina mountains where she grew Jurassic-Park sized vegetables. I asked her one day how she did it.

"Chicken droppings," she said dryly. "A garden won't grow right without it."

It took a few years after that to really enjoy a tomato out of her garden again. But I never forgot the lesson: It's the messy, unpleasant stuff that grows a great garden. Just like sometimes it's the messy stuff in life, the mistakes and wrong turns, that grows a rich existence. Yet we bemoan every tiny mistake. We begin to define ourselves by the wrong turns.

I think of my first Good Friday service as the new sen-ior pastor at Madison Avenue Baptist Church in New York City. I was so focused and worried about the upcoming ser-mon, I forgot the words to the Lord's Prayer. Literally.

> "Lead us not into ... *um* ... the valley ... of the shadow of death? Because ... *um* ... it's a bad place—that val-ley. Thank you? Forever and ever amen."

Needless to say, there were some confused looks as the congregation raised their heads after the prayer. For the rest of the time, I sat behind the pulpit contemplating what other careers I might pursue. As the service ended, one of our senior members came up to me and said, "Well, I've never heard the Lord's Prayer done that way, but it sure made me sit up and listen!"

You never know what growth and learning will come from a mistake. You can never fully rise to your potential until you shed some of the negative baggage that weighs you down. Pick your eyes up off the floor, for that's not where you'll find life's great opportunities for joy.

The World's Greatest Buffet

"A sad soul can kill you quicker, far quicker, than
a germ."

—JOHN STEINBECK, AMERICAN WRITER

Besides the Rice Krispies Treats, one of my other childhood culinary treats was the rare celebratory occasion when we would go to the all-you-can-eat Shoney's breakfast bar. This was no ordinary buffet. It spread as far as the eye could see (or at least the eyes of a six-year-old).

Of course, there were the requisite Southern staples: scrambled eggs, bacon, sausage (link and patty), biscuits with milk gravy, grits with butter and melted Velveeta slices, sweet buns, coffee cake, and doughnuts. The usual.

What set this buffet apart, however, was not the breakfast buffet, but the dessert bar that, after 10 a.m., was also included. Big vats of chocolate and vanilla pudding, Cool Whip, and ice cream. Pancakes, bacon, *and* pudding? It was too fabulous to believe.

There was, however, a tragic twist. Here at the world's greatest buffet, you were only offered a salad plate on which to eat. And I couldn't really compensate by making fifty trips, as my mother considered it rude to get up multiple times at an all-you-can-eat. It was an ugly reality: At the world's greatest breakfast/dessert buffet, I was able to enjoy only about 1 percent of the offerings.

I have since ceased eating pancakes, bacon, and pudding for breakfast (at least on most days). But the lesson still rings true: Every day we wake up, we are offered the world's greatest buffet. It spreads as far as the eye can see with vats of pleasure and joy, laughter and smiles, happiness and contentment. It is available to all. It is bought and paid for. Yet we take only a tiny salad plate to this fabulous spread and serve ourselves a few mere morsels. We're already stuffed with so much else that there's no room for joy.

We trump every opportunity for joy with our overscheduled Blackberry calendars and our thirty-page "to-do" lists. We attempt to chase down some sense of worth by overachieving and overworking. We worship at the altar of multi-tasking: running errands in the car while chatting on the cell phone, checking the GPS, flipping the XM stations, and scribbling the grocery list on our windshield notepad. In the end we are left with nothing but a tiny salad plate (if that) for the great buffet of joy.

About the only thing we consciously make room for is worry. Ironically, *worry* is an Anglo-Saxon word meaning "to strangle" or "to choke." Like the kudzu vine that grows in the South, worry grows fast and wild, cutting off our emotional and spiritual light. In the end, we lose the very ability to see the beauty and joy around us.

"The most wasted day is one without laughter."

—E. E. CUMMINGS, AMERICAN POET AND ESSAYIST

A few years back, a nondescript young man in jeans, a t-shirt, and a baseball cap sat down in a Washington, D.C., Metro station and began to play music on his violin. Thousands of commuters hurried by with not even a glance. Unknown to the hurried masses, however, this was no ordinary street vendor. In fact, it was Joshua Bell, one of the finest classical musicians in the world, playing some of the most beautiful and intricate pieces ever written on a $3.5 million dollar violin. The event was organized by the *Washington Post* as a social experiment on people's priorities. Clearly, we failed.

We are surrounded by a smorgasbord of joy and happiness. With every new day, there is the miracle of life and energy and spirit. Yet we march through life missing most of it, allowing ourselves only the few insignificant morsels we believe we deserve.

I say it's time for a revolt. Let's storm the kitchen and demand some bigger plates! Remember those women on the Titanic? Remember Pluto? What are you waiting for? Laugh now and don't be skimpy about it. Like the stewed tomatoes, life goes down a lot easier if you if nibble on some dessert with it.

REFLECTIONS

Do you believe you deserve happiness? If your answer is no, why not?

What things have been said to you to make you feel that way? (You may need extra paper for this ...) Who told you? What did they tell you? Are *they* happy? What in their lives do you think made them say it?

Have you ever felt plutoed? When?

Do you make time for joy? Do you schedule it in? Do you prioritize it in your life? Do you pick up a salad plate or a dinner plate when it comes to joy and laughter? What could you do to make more room for joy? (Remember the Titanic ...)

PART II

What Would Happen If We Laughed?

"Laughter's the nearest we ever get, or should get, to sainthood. It's the state of grace that saves most of us from contempt."

—JOHN OSBORNE, ENGLISH PLAYWRIGHT

5 High Places of the Heart

Finding Perspective through Laughter

A New Way to See

> "Life is a tragedy when seen in close-up, but a comedy in long-shot."
>
> —CHARLIE CHAPLIN, ENGLISH COMIC ACTOR

I've done many crazy things in my life but there are two that stick out: performing stand-up and climbing Mount Kilimanjaro. Both were intimidating. And both made me throw up. But there's a third similarity (and this is the reason I attempted either of these crazy things): both comedy and Kilimanjaro provide high places—places that bring an entirely new sense of perspective.

From the time we are toddlers, we are constantly trying to find high places in order to see. We wail until we're put in the high chair so we can see everyone at the table. We beg to be put on the shoulders of a tall person so we can see the parade. We scamper up the branches of a towering tree in order to spy on our next-door neighbor.

As adults, we continue the same quest. We peer out of observation towers atop high buildings. We gaze at the world through satellite cameras. And a few crazy people (like myself) climb tall mountains.

But you don't have to climb Kilimanjaro to get a new perspective. You can just as easily get those same lessons in the daily chaos at ground level. You just need to find a high place of the heart.

Helium for the Heart

"Nobody can be uncheered with a balloon."

—WINNIE THE POOH

The spirit of the human heart is basically a balloon in disguise. *Not* the lame sculpted-into-a-wiener-dog kind of balloon. I mean the tied-to-a-string, high-soaring, helium kind of balloon.

As a kid, I would get a helium balloon every year at the Festival in the Park held near our house. There was something transporting about holding the string of one of these maverick spheres that refused to be held down by earth or gravity. I would carry it proudly around the park, then carefully back to my room where I would tie it to my white French provincial desk chair.

When I awoke the next day, the balloon would be there bouncing happily back and forth in front of the heat vent. When I'd get home from school, it would still be there, just lower and less active. That night it could barely hover above the chair, the string itself beginning to weigh the balloon down. And by the second morning, it would be lying on the floor, completely deflated and a fraction of its original size.

Anyone who has ever watched the life cycle of a helium balloon has also seen the full range of the human heart. When lightened, the heart soars upward, flying above all earthly constraints. When saddened and heavy, it deflates, sinks, bounces along the ground, shrinking to a fraction of its original size. Like any balloon, all it needs is a good dose of helium to get it soaring again. And the best helium for the human heart is humor.

When we laugh, we take our eyes off ourselves and our problems, even if only for a brief moment. It's in that brief moment that we are freed of our daily worries, that we become lightened—in mood and in spirit. And, like a great helium balloon, we rise up and float above the concerns of our world below.

I think when people say "Laugh it up," they mean it—literally. Laughter empowers the human heart to fly. When we laugh, our hearts find high places. And when we are in high places, whether on the slopes of Kilimanjaro or at home, we see the world differently. Up high, the world looks less scary. Up high, we gain a sense of appreciation. Up high, we can see our way through.

A View from Kilimanjaro

"It is your attitude, not your aptitude, that determines your altitude."

—ZIG ZIGLAR, AUTHOR AND MOTIVATIONAL SPEAKER

Day one of the Kilimanjaro climb, I cried. How could I not? My last hike had been up Kings Mountain State Park, a towering 850 feet. Kilimanjaro was 19,340 feet. I had taken Delta flights that cruised at lower altitudes.

As scary as the climb seemed, the prospect of staying in our base camp was even scarier. As we drove into our Serengeti camp, we passed every imaginable carnivore: lions, hyenas, crocodiles. They peered at us out of the bush as if we were medium-rare burgers and someone had just yelled "order up!" And we were going to sleep among them tonight! All that stood between me and certain death was a flimsy little canvas tent and, of course, my Swiss Army knife, featuring a blade that doubled as a fingernail file.

Confirming my fears were the parting words of our guide, Kampanya, before we turned in for the evening: "If you get up in the middle of the night, make sure to shine your light around first. If you see large yellow eyes, don't go." Not shockingly, I stayed in my tent.

Thankfully I lived, and the next morning we began our climb approximately 2,000 feet above the plains into the forests on the lower slopes of the mountain. Throughout the day, I thought about those hungry lions. The higher I got, the less scary they seemed. Two thousand feet of altitude and separation does a lot for one's courage. By the time we got to camp, the lions were a distant memory. At least the hungry lions found in the Serengeti.

Of course, there were still the hungry lions I faced back home. After the trip, I knew I would return to job pressures, financial worries, family and relationship issues—all the things that sit outside our tents, ready to eat us alive. Of course, we can climb up and away from them, like on the slopes of Kilimanjaro. We just need a little altitude between us and them.

Up High, the World Seems Less Scary

"You cannot overestimate the unimportance of practically everything."
—GOODMAN ACE, AMERICAN HUMORIST AND COMEDY WRITER

In the sixteenth century, the great astronomer Copernicus advanced the ground-breaking theory that the earth was not the center of the universe. You certainly wouldn't know it today. We each believe that everything in this great universe revolves around us and our concerns. *My* job is the hardest, *my* quotas are the highest, *my* boss is the most heinous, *my* customer is the most difficult, *my* family is the most annoying, *my* child is the most trying, *my* disappointments are the worst.

One of the things that used to scare me the most as a new minister was what to say during hospital visits. What if I said the wrong thing? What if they asked me something I couldn't answer? (As if there are any answers to be offered in a hospital.) The minister I worked for at the time told me a story that completely changed my perspective.

One day he made a hospital visit to a particularly prickly congregation member. Sadly, she was dying and was in and out of consciousness. As he sat by her bed holding her hand, suddenly she began saying, "Please don't leave me. Please stay with me."

"I wasn't sure what to say," Mike told me, "so I just managed something like 'I'm right here, Ilse. I'm not leaving you.'"

Ilse opened her eyes, looked right at him and, with a disgusted look, said, "I'm not talking to *you*! I'm talking to *Him*!" And she pointed to the crucifix on the hospital wall.

It helps to be reminded where we fit into the great scheme of things. As author Anne Lamott wrote, "Only one six-billionth of this is about you."

And that's just in relation to other humans. Remember that ferrets and warthogs were created before us in Genesis. And God's furry and scaly creatures have done way better on the evolution path than we have. A salmon with the brain the size of a Milk Dud can find its way home a thousand miles away. And we, in our fancy, digital, high-tech world, still need a GPS to get to the grocery store.

Think about how much we worry about the things that growl outside our tent. It's funny, really. The fact is, it doesn't matter how much we do or how many problems we solve or what we overcome in this lifetime, the size of our funeral will always depend solely on the weather. If only we would laugh a little bit, we might smarten up. At least we would get a little perspective on ourselves—one where our hungry lions look a little less scary.

Up High, We Can Appreciate the Little Things

"Angels can fly because they take themselves lightly."
—G. K. CHESTERTON, ENGLISH WRITER AND JOURNALIST

Day four of the climb, around 15,000 feet, I started feeling sick. And this was not the kind of sick where you just pop down to CVS for Pepto-Bismol. This was the kind of sick where you pray for an express bus to the Mayo Clinic. Like a freight train, this massive headache hit, soon followed by violent dizziness and nausea.

Based on my extensive medical knowledge gleaned from Fodor's *The Complete African Safari Planner,* I *knew* that I had developed a cerebral edema from the altitude and would die within the hour. As I tried to remember who I left what to in my will, Kampanya appeared, handed me some antinausea pills and a bottle of filtered water with electrolytes, assuring me that it was routine altitude sickness and that death was not imminent.

I popped the pills, drank the water, and slowly continued the last mile to our camp at about 15,500 feet. It was an arduous last mile. I'd take a few steps, stop to catch my breath, kneel down, throw up, stand up, repeat.

Illness or not, altitude forces you to slow down, to become aware of your surroundings, your breathing, and every move you make. Unlike home, where I scurried around like a mall speed walker, here I was forced to go at a pace that allowed me to observe things.

While kneeling on the ground gasping for breath, I noticed things I had missed earlier in the day. Things like tiny azure alpine flowers; vivid green lichen and moss in between the rocks on the path; so many things I had missed along the journey because I had been focused on the race of getting up the mountain. If moss and lichen are what I missed on Kilimanjaro, then how much more must I be missing rushing around at sea level? And I know I'm not alone in this. We all rush through life, missing so much of its meaning and beauty.

We just need to make time to laugh. Like the mandatory slow pace at high altitudes, laughter slows us down and brings us back to the present moment.

"Days pass, and years vanish and we walk sightless among miracles."

—JEWISH PRAYER

We have all faked listening to another person with superficial head nods, the ubiquitous "um hum" thrown in periodically. But a nod and an' "um hum" won't cut it for humor. You cannot multitask and laugh at the same time. You can only laugh when you are fully listening.

That's why I use humor in sermons. Every Sunday about halfway through my delivery, I can see people's gaze start to change, their minds beginning to spin through pressing outside concerns: Where should we go for brunch after the service? Did I turn off the burner at home? What time is that meeting on Monday morning? Where did I park the car?

That's about the time I throw in an unexpected twist. Like the time during a Lenten sermon when I was bemoaning our lack of faith.

"You know, Christians could sure learn a thing or two from Elvis fans. 'Cause these people have *no* doubt that the King lives."

The people who were listening laughed. The people who weren't listening, looked up blankly, then turned to their neighbors and whispered, "What did I miss?"

There is value in staying in the moment, noticing the little things around us. Most of the important things in life are not "out there," but right under our noses.

Growing up, I had an aunt who felt a need to verbalize everything she saw out the car window.

"Oh, look, there's a tree."

"Look! There's a parking lot."

"Look! There's a leaf."

It drove us all crazy. Yet over the years, I have come to see the value of noticing what's right in front of us. There are things of great beauty that will feed our souls: a beautiful sunrise, the way the sunlight hits an autumn tree, a tiny green spec popping out of plowed dirt in a new garden.

There are also things that demand our attention, but get lost in the chaos: a twinge of sadness in a loved one's voice, a look of loneliness in the eye of a passerby, an expression of defeat on a stranger's face.

The Buddha tells a parable about a man who was shot by a poisoned arrow. Rather than allow his servants to pull out the arrow, he demanded to find out who shot it, why they shot it, what type of poison was on the arrow, and what type of arrow it was. In the meantime, he died because he didn't deal with what was right in front of him.

The point of the parable is clear: Don't lose the things that pine for our attention in this life. Like those little azure flowers on the trail, these are the things that most deserve our attention. Here is where the work is. Here is where our blessings are. We need only to look, listen, and laugh.

Up High, We Can See Our Way Through

> "Today is your day. Your mountain is waiting. So ... get on your way."
>
> —Dr. Seuss

The night before the summit, I was curled up in my down sleeping bag in a whirling snowstorm at 18,000 feet. At least I wasn't throwing up, but I was still fighting a headache, *and* still dizzy, *and* still out of breath (even lying in my sleeping bag). Given that we were now in the middle of a blizzard, I decided enough was enough. I was going to descend.

I crawled out and headed for Kampanya's tent. As I was rehearsing my I-really-need-to-descend-now speech, I looked out across the ledge on which we were camped. Through the blowing snow I could see the same storm hammering the base of Kilimanjaro not with snow but with lightning and thunder. Past the storm clouds, I could see the moon and stars in a crystal clear sky over the plains far beyond. We were so high that even while in the storm, I could see the calm coming after the storm. I decided to crawl back into my tent and give it another try.

It's too bad we can't always see through the storms and problems of life. Whether it is a crisis at work or a relationship breakdown, if we can get some altitude, some laughter, we can usually see our way through.

During my tenure as a banking lawyer, I was in a meeting with our technology group regarding a system glitch that caused inappropriate dunning notices to be generated to many of our card members. There were intricate flow charts on the walls, thick manuals spread across the table, and half the PhDs on the planet in the room. Still, no one could figure out how to fix the computer.

Finally, one young employee said in a tentative voice, "How about we just unplug it?"

After a moment of stunned silence, everyone started laughing. The discussions that followed were much freer and more creative. Within thirty minutes, a solution was found, and, ironically, it related to the power.

Laughter is a source of creativity. Studies have shown that the mind associates more broadly, connects more easily, and sees more solutions when people laugh. We find jokes or comments funny because they juxtapose seemingly unrelated things or ideas. And that's creativity: putting things together in a unique way. When we think creatively, we are more productive and more readily able to solve problems.

It's similar to shielding the sun. When you look at an object in direct sunlight, you see it in a limited, hazy way. But when you shield the sun with your hand, the objects you are looking at become clear in a way you hadn't seen.

Whatever storm or problem comes at us, if we can climb our way to a laugh, we can usually see our way through.

"You don't stop laughing because you grow old. You grow old because you stop laughing."

—MICHAEL PRITCHARD, COMEDIAN AND SPEAKER

Since the day I returned from that trip, I have kept a photo on my desk of me on the slopes of Kilimanjaro the morning after that snowstorm. I look pretty beat up, but quite happy. I have the expression of someone who has seen life's problems from a new perspective; someone who has begun to notice the little things; someone who has seen her way through the storm. I keep it to remind me of the view from that high mountain. Most of all, I keep it to preserve that high place of the heart.

REFLECTIONS

What are the three scariest things on your desk or in your life today? Do any of these things get to the core issues of life? Health? Food? Shelter? In twenty years, will you care?* What clues do your answers give you about your need to lighten up?

---

*I'm assuming the answer is no. However, if it's yes, take a preview look at chapter 9. This one's for you.

Humor is about juxtaposing two opposing ideas, such as the amount of stress and energy we spend on issues that really don't deserve it. Think about these combinations:

- Picture a time you worried about things over which you had no control.
- Remember a moment where you dragged around heavy loads of anger over the lightest and slightest of things.
- Recall a night where you stayed awake with fear over something that never happened.

Can you see the humor here? Are you laughing? If not, keep thinking.

If you allowed laughter into the difficult places of life, what things might you see that you are now missing? Things with your family? A clearer sense of priorities? How do these things rank when compared to the problems that obscured them?

6 We're All Hells Angels
Using Humor to See Past Our Differences

Too Funny to Believe

"Before you criticize someone you should walk a mile in their shoes. That way, when you criticize them, you're a mile away and you have their shoes."

— JACK HANDEY, AMERICAN HUMORIST

The Motel 6 or the Sea and Sand Lodge? Located conveniently by a Kentucky Fried Chicken, the Motel 6 offered the more appropriate oasis. Besides, in landlocked Montana the name "Sea and Sand" seemed somewhat suspect. Such are the critical decisions required on a cross-country motorcycle trip.

Harley owners for decades, my partner,* Toby, and I only recently ventured into cross-country riding. We completed our first trip, from Wisconsin to South Dakota, in a leisurely six days,

---

*I'm waiting for Webster's to come up with a better term for long-term relationships. *Partner* sounds suspiciously like we own a Wendy's franchise. But after age thirty, *boyfriend* sounds too close to a prom date, and *significant other* has too many syllables.

wearing only jeans, Harley t-shirts, and leather jackets. Now, four years later, we were on a fifteen-day ride from New York City to British Columbia, sporting fringed chaps, chains, skull jewelry, and tattoos of rattle snakes wrapped around swords.

On the surface, we were pretty fierce: dirt laden, leather-and-chain-wearing outlaws roaring up on a huge, black cherry-colored Harley Davidson with inordinately loud custom pipes. Had anyone looked closely, however, they might have seen the cracks in the outlaw façade.

I was sporting bright red nail polish, not something usually worn by the Hells Angels. Other clues included the fact that my tattoos were adhesive and Toby's leather jacket patches included not just skulls, but a Harvard emblem and the mascot from a prep school in Connecticut.

But no one looked. No one cared. We were mainstream yuppies masquerading as Hells Angels. We loved it because we could live it and then leave it. Or so we thought.

The desk clerk at the motel looked up as we walked in. Surveying our rather grimy exterior, she abruptly said, "I'm sorry, we're full."

I pointed to the empty parking lot.

"Really?" I asked.

She shook her head, "We're *full*."

I started laughing. "Oh, this is like some funny hidden camera thing, right?"

"No," she replied coldly, "we just don't rent to *your* type."

"And what type might that be?" I asked.

"Bikers," she said with great distain and returned to her paperwork.

I began laughing so hard I started coughing. Toby, an ex-prosecutor, and me, a Baptist minister ... dangerous outlaws? Too funny to believe.

"I'm not a biker," I said between gasps for air. "I'm just a Baptist minister on vacation."

She frowned, shook her head, and with great deliberation said, "The Bible says it's wrong to lie."

By the vise grip on my arm, I knew Toby feared a very "un-minister" retort. Refusing the tempting response, we slunk off to the suspect, yet biker-friendly, Sea and Sand.

Whatever Happened to "Love Thy Neighbor"?

"Love your crooked neighbor, with your own crooked heart."

—W. H. AUDEN, ANGLO-AMERICAN POET

"I can't believe that woman," I muttered to Toby later that evening, as I chewed on a KFC wing. "Whatever happened to 'love thy neighbor'?"

Toby shot me a skeptical look.

"Okay, okay," I admitted, as I remembered all the times that day that I, too, had judged people unfairly—like the people in the car who had cut us off outside of Billings, Montana.

"What do you expect?" I had shouted to Toby with disgust from the back of the bike. "They have Jersey plates."

Earlier that day there had also been that bike next to the one open parking space at the Dairy Queen in Miles City.

"Do we have to park *here*?" I had said, rolling my eyes. "I don't want to be seen near a Suzuki."

Of course, we had encountered the lowest of all people at a rest area near Terry, Montana: those who towed their bike on a trailer behind their Winnebago. Toby and I had simply exchanged contempt-filled glances.

Unfortunately, I had more in common with my new "friend" at the desk of the Motel 6 than I wanted to admit. In our defense, however, judging others is hardly a unique trait. Like the ranges with the barbed-wire fences we had been riding past, human beings seem instinctively to draw boundaries, to see the differences first.

We judge on the slightest things: skin color, weight, ethnicity, and gender—things, unlike our biker gear, that cannot be removed.

Ironic, given that scientists in mapping the human gene have determined that human beings are in fact 99.99 percent genetically the same. Religion, skin color, ethnicity, national origin, gender—none of these matter. We are 99.99 percent the same. Which means that our judgments of each other— our injustice, our violence, our warfare—are all over this .01 percent difference.

It appears that we need a new way of seeing things. We need a tool to bridge our perceived differences.

Humor Is the WD40 and Duct Tape of Life

"If you haven't got anything nice to say about anybody, come sit next to me!"

—ALICE ROOSEVELT LONGWORTH,
PRESIDENT THEODORE ROOSEVELT'S OLDEST CHILD

The next morning, we began the daily ritual of repacking the bike. It was particularly difficult as we were on the last leg of our trip and had a number of new Harley t-shirts to stuff in the pack. As I shoved the last one in, I heard a troubling rip-ping sound. The bike pack had begun to split.

"Where's the duct tape?" I sighed.

As Toby tried to lift the pack off to inspect the damage, we realized that the pack clips had rusted to the backrest.

"I hope it's with the WD40," he said, rolling his eyes.

What would we do without these? The old saying is true: In life, the only two tools you need are WD40 and duct tape. That is because all of life's problems break down into one of two categories: something moves and it shouldn't, or it doesn't move and it should. That is true for everything from motorcy-cle packs to relationships.

Unless you are a contractor, most people don't carry duct tape and WD40 with them on a daily basis. However, there is another tool that each of us carries that performs the exact same tasks: humor.

Humor is the WD40 and duct tape of life. Like WD40 on those rusted clips, humor jars us loose, breaks us open, and makes us see things in a fresh, new way. And like the duct tape on the pack, it bonds us together by highlighting our commonalities.

Is This Some Kind of Joke?

"One out of every four Americans is suffering from some form of mental illness. Think of your three best friends. If they're okay, then it's you."

—RITA MAE BROWN, AMERICAN AUTHOR

There are many things in our lives that get stuck at an early age. Some of them are good—like an addiction to chili cheese Fritos or a love of ACC basketball. Some, however, are not so good—such as preconceived notions about others who are different. Like a jack-in-the-box, generalizations and prejudices sit tucked away in our heart chambers until we encounter someone who matches the profile then, "POP!"—they come jumping out.

I encountered this myself as a Southerner living north of the Mason-Dixon Line. The second I use *y'all* to refer to one person, people smile with this "isn't that quaint" look and then scan the room for someone with an accent nearer to Robert DeNiro in *Taxi Driver*. Apparently, phrases such as "ah yoo tawkin' ta me?" imply intellect.

But sometimes we face stereotypes that are harder to break than a Southern accent.

Former Senator Barry Goldwater told the story about being born to a Jewish father and an Episcopalian mother. In visiting a golf club where they wouldn't let Jews play, he asked, "I'm only half Jewish. Can I play nine holes?"

Humor is like verbal Aikido, a Japanese martial art form where the focus is not on striking an opponent but on using your opponent's energy to gain control or to throw them off balance. It also may have been what Jesus meant when he said, "Turn the other cheek" (Matthew 5:39). In combat, turning the other cheek avoids a backhand blow, usually the more powerful of the strikes.

One cold, icy morning, I was sitting at my desk in Queens. The phone rang. It was a plaintiff's attorney threatening to sue the bank where I worked. As I listened to him rant, I shuffled through my in-box and found his draft complaint. Skimming it over, my eyes fell on the court listed at the top: District Court of Honolulu.

"Excuse me," I interrupted. "I would love for you to sue me."

Silence.

"In fact, I wish you'd do it today. And put it on the fast track for trial."

More silence.

"Is this some kind of joke?" he finally said.

"Not at all," I said sweetly (with a thick Southern accent). "I am sitting in an office looking out at an ice storm in Queens. You're threatening to take me to trial in a courthouse looking out at Waikiki. Please, *please* sue me."

After a moment of more silence, he started to laugh. Then we both laughed. In ten minutes we had settled the case.

When we face conflict with humor, the power shifts, perceptions are jarred, and we begin to see things in a fresh way. Like tilling hard ground, laughter opens us to new ways of seeing and breaks us free of those places we are stuck.

We All Laugh in the Same Language

"Do not neglect to show hospitality to strangers, for by doing that some have entertained angels without knowing it."

—HEBREWS 13:2

One of my favorite parts of being a stand-up is performing with my friend Bob Alper, a rabbi who is a stand-up comedian, and a group of Muslim comedians from a troop called "Allah Made Me Funny." After 9/11, Bob and several of these comedians went on the road with an interfaith comedy show that addressed the difficult cultural and religious issues facing the world.

Each offered stories from his own perspective.

Ahmad Ahmad explained to the audience his experience of being a Muslim in an airport: "Most people have to be at the airport two hours before their flight. For me, it's three months."

Bob shared the differences in language and culture: "On my first visit to Jerusalem, I was eager to try out my classical Hebrew. While riding in a cab, I asked the driver to stop at the next corner. He looked at me funny; then I realized what I had said was not 'let me off here,' but 'BEHOLD! Here I descend!'"

The audiences in our shows span every imaginable faith: Jews, Christians, Muslims, atheist, agnostics, Buddhists, Hindus. And for two short hours, the differences are forgotten, and we all laugh together.

Like a good roll of duct tape, humor bonds us to each other. It strengthens us as a community, and it allows us to transcend our differences and our barriers. When we laugh with someone—whether it is a stranger, a friend, a lover, or an enemy—our worlds overlap for a tiny, but significant moment. It is then that defenses are lowered, ideas and feelings are shared, and the best in each other gleams forth.

Only when we can get past ourselves, when we can laugh past our perceived superiority and righteousness, can we truly look at our neighbor with a sense of hospitality and justice. The author Peggy Noonan once said, "We all weep in the same language." We all laugh in the same language as well. When we laugh together, we not only cross barriers, but we also bond together as community.

A few years ago, I spent some time camping in a redwood forest in northern California. (A holy pilgrimage if I've ever had one.) Living up to two thousand years, these monu-mental trees grow up to four hundred feet in height (compa-rable to a thirty-five-story building). But they don't reach these towering heights by sinking their roots down into the ground. They grow to these heights by sending their roots *out*—horizontally—and connecting with the other trees in the forest.

So much pain in our world today—terrorism, violence, war—stems from deep canyons of separation that divide cul-tures, nations, even families. When diverse voices and faces come together through laughter, we connect at a deeper level, like those trees at root level. We become a bit stronger. We become a bit taller. We bear each other up.

There's a Little Hell in Every Angel and a Little Angel in Every Hell

> "The one important thing I've learned over the years is the difference between taking one's work seriously and one's self seriously. The first is imperative; the second is disastrous."
>
> —DAME MARGOT FONTEYN, ENGLISH BALLERINA

After our WD40 and duct-tape repairs, I decided to make yet one more visit to my friend the desk clerk at the Motel 6. When I walked in, she showed a vague look of recollection that quickly changed to shock when I laid my business card reading "Rev. Susan G. Sparks, Senior Pastor" on the counter. As she stared at the card, I leaned over the counter, tapped it with my finger, and said, "The Bible also says 'judge not,'" and smiled.

We stood there in silence. Then I started laughing. She stared at me in surprise and slowly smiled.

"I guess there's a little Hells Angels in all of us," she said. Then we both laughed.

She was right, you know. We all carry a little "hell" *and* a little "angel" inside of us. In order to truly love ourselves and our neighbor, we have to acknowledge both aspects within. That sense of awareness is clearest when we find a way to laugh—at ourselves and our frail human judgments and limitations. It is in the laughter that we not only discover ourselves, but our common bonds with those we would least expect.

REFLECTIONS

Think of someone whom you have judged unfairly. Can you think of what you have in common with them? What might the two of you be able to laugh about together? Families? Kids? Work? Traffic? If you laughed together, how might that change your perception of each other?

Recall a time you laughed with someone you didn't know. Maybe it was in a meeting or in an elevator or someone on television. Did you feel more of a sense of connection with them? Would you go so far to say that you were more invested in their well-being?

Think of a recent conflict you've had. Was there anything about the situation that could have made you or the other person laugh? How might that have changed the dynamics and/or results of the situation? Where might you be able to use laughter to diffuse a tough situation, to "turn the other cheek"?

7 Burping in the Pulpit

Rediscovering a Fresh Spiritual Practice through the Eyes of a Child

Left, Right. Left, Right.

> "It takes a very long time to become young."
> —PABLO PICASSO, SPANISH PAINTER

We have all been there, that point in life where we suddenly realize that we have heard it all before: the stories, the jokes, the news, the lessons. We hope and pray for something new, but it's the same thing day in and day out. Things that once were interesting, now aren't; things that once excited us, don't; and things that used to make us smile, can't. One foot in front of the other. Left, right. Left, right.

I hit that point a while back when I was faced with preaching yet *another* a sermon on Jonah and the whale. Seriously, how many times can you tell this story?

You've probably heard it all before: God tells Jonah to preach a fiery message of repentance to the Ninevites—the

Ninevites who were known for skinning their enemies. Jonah thinks about it for approximately three seconds and says, "I think not" and bolts. Ultimately, he ends up on a boat with a bunch of Mediterranean pirates who fling him into the sea where he gets swallowed by a whale. Jonah tells God he's sorry, God makes the whale belch him out on a beach, and Jonah heads off to his destiny to annoy the Ninevites. Yup. Got it.

The only way to refresh this well-worn story was to find someone who hadn't heard it before (or at least had heard it only three or four times). A children's sermon, perhaps? The story would still be fresh to them. So, let them tell it—maybe even change around the characters a bit.

Fast forward to Sunday morning. I invited the children of the congregation up front to join me for the sermon.

"So, who knows the story of Jonah and the whale?" I asked.

"OOOO!" "OOOh!" A sea of little hands shot up.

"Good for you!" I smiled. "But, I have a harder question. Who knows the whale's side of the story?"

There was silence for a moment, then Ranger,* the more creative of our posse of wee folk, shot up his hand.

"I know, I know!"

"Well, Ranger, would you like to share with everyone?" (Mistake #1)

"Yes!"

"Then let's you and I go to the pulpit so you can tell us this story." (Mistake #2)

I took Ranger by the hand, led him to the pulpit, then set him upon a chair so everyone could see him. I pulled the microphone down to his level so everyone could hear him. (Mistake #3)

---

*Name changed to protect the innocent.

"Now, Ranger, tell us how the whale would tell the story of Jonah."

Ranger smiled out at the congregation, leaned in as close as he could possibly get to the microphone, then let out a prolonged, noisy burp that echoed throughout the sanctuary.

Stunned silence. No one had ever burped in that great mahogany pulpit before. And from the sea of contorted, shock-filled faces, I understood why.

We hung in that precarious moment of shock until, finally, Ranger let out a squeal of laughter in celebration of his great coup. Soon the other kids around the pulpit began to laugh. Then the entire congregation. It was a great laugh of relief—relief that none of us had been struck by lightning for that deliciously edgy liturgical moment. More than that, it was a laugh of relief because something new and wonderful and spontaneous had just happened.

Ranger at the Helm

> "Only by assuming a playful attitude toward our religious
> tradition can we possibly make any sense of it."
>
> —HARVEY COX, PROFESSOR, HARVARD DIVINITY SCHOOL

One of my favorite questions to ask people is, "At your playful best, what age do you see yourself?"

Personally, I see myself at seven. I have a photo of me at seven, standing with my parents on the porch of my grandparent's farm. I am in an outfit I obviously hated; obviously, because I had this clear expression of "yuck" on my face. But it was "yuck" overlaid with a sly, mischievous smile, as if I had something fun and rebellious planned to make up for my obvious oppression. There is something so true in that photo, something spot-on to my personality. Every time I look at it, I know I will always be seven at heart.

Unfortunately, as an adult, my seven-year-old self often gets shooed away in favor of more appropriate formalities and *gravitas*. I've seen the consequences of this kind of suppression in far too many adults. We're told in so many ways that our mischievous, playful side has no place in our serious adult world; and it certainly has no place in our serious adult spiritual lives. Yet when we exclude the child within, our religion, like our lives, becomes rote and dull. We begin to believe that we have heard it all before: all the stories, all the scripture, all the lessons. Things that once were interesting, now aren't; things that once excited us, don't; things that used to make us smile, can't. Left, right. Left, right.

> "Keep me away from the wisdom which does not cry, the philosophy which does not laugh, and the greatness which does not bow before children."
>
> —KAHLIL GIBRAN, LEBANESE-AMERICAN AUTHOR

What would happen if we brought that little kid in all of us back? What if Ranger was at the helm of our spiritual lives? We might rediscover a sense of spontaneity, a feeling of spiritual honesty and intimacy, and a capacity for fun and festivity—things we didn't even remembered existed.

You Gotta Get Real

> "The Christian church has all the language of a party, but hasn't been able to pull it off."
>
> —CAL SAMRA, AUTHOR

Enter majestic organ music ...

The service begins. A sense of grandeur and other-worldliness settles over the congregation. Pastoral, bucolic music wafts through the pristine sanctuary filled with glittering gold, towering stained glass, and well-adorned guests. Suddenly, a squeal pierces through the holiness. A tiny child has spotted the pink, furry hippo dangling above her head in her stroller and explodes with glee. Heads turn. Scowls emerge. What doth dare interrupt the solemnity of worship?

Oh, come on. You don't remember doing this? You don't remember the early times in your life when all the primal instincts freely came out—anger, tears, joy, and laughter? The times when there were no trappings of adulthood, like self-doubt, cynicism, or defensiveness? The times when, if you felt it, you showed it?

Childhood was an era of pure spontaneity. If we thought something was funny, we laughed until milk came out of our nose. If we loved someone, there was no simple peck on the cheek. We would come tearing out of the house with our arms open, yelling, "Yeah, you're home!"

We loved before we feared. We were curious before we were threatened. We accepted before we judged (unless, of course, it was a vegetable).

> "We spend the first twelve months of our children's lives teaching them to walk and talk, and the next twelve years telling them to sit down and shut up."
>
> —PHYLLIS DILLER, ACTRESS AND COMEDIAN

But here we are as adults, clinging to our stale, rote, safe places. We prefer schedules to interruptions, predictability to spontaneity, plastic to the real thing.*

Spontaneity is risky. But so is real life. We live in a world where we can't predict what will happen next. Life has no script. So why not worship as we live?

One of the things that scares me most as a comedian are hecklers. They are unpredictable, they come out of nowhere, and you have no idea when or how they will strike. Much to my dismay, I have found they are not limited to dark, smoky comedy clubs.

Today I have my own in-house church heckler, Charlie McCarthy. And yes, this is his real name. At ninety-eight years old (going on seven), Charlie has lived long enough that he feels comfortable saying what he wants whenever the mood strikes. In the middle of a song, he'll shout, "I just love the choir!" In the middle of my prayer, he'll interrupt with what he believes is a more important request, such as, "Lord, please bless the Mets. They need it. Amen." Spontaneity is not something Charlie fears.

Every Sunday, Charlie worships as he lives. He grounds us all in the gritty realness of our humanity. He gives permission to feel, to react, and to be ourselves.

I am not suggesting we all shout out Mets prayers during odd times in our sacred rituals (unless, of course, you are a Mets fan). What I am suggesting is that we attempt to feel again.

In our information-driven society, we have lost much of our ability to perceive and experience. We have become too

---

*An interesting statistic for doubters: plastic pink flamingos now outnumber real ones.

dependent on outside interpretation. As Viola Spolin, a pioneer in improvisational theater, said, we have learned to "see with each others' eyes and smell with others' noses." Spontaneity empowers a more independent sense of experience; it allows us to generate feelings from within, not feelings directed from the outside.

I am the daughter of a woman who was an amazing gardener. Unfortunately, I am also very lazy, which means my poor little plant wards don't get the consistent care they deserve. I had a trailing verbena, for instance, that was in the same pot for years. Finally, it began to die, and I asked my mom, "What's with the plant? I watered it."

"Susan," she said looking at me with disbelief, "living things need room to grow. Shake out the roots a little bit and give it a bigger pot."

Sure enough, when I pulled it out, the roots had grown around each other in a tiny, tight ball, strangling out any water or nourishment. Within a day or two of replanting in a new spacious pot, it popped right back to life.

"It is never too late to have a happy childhood."
—TOM ROBBINS, AMERICAN AUTHOR

If our spiritual path is to have any life, it needs to be shaken out a bit and given room to grow. Laughter tends to do just that. It shakes up our "roots" and brings air and energy into tired, worn souls. If we give ourselves permission to feel and play and laugh on our own terms, who knows—we might learn something new.

A Real Live Chat with God

"Laughter is the beginning of prayer."
—REINHOLD NIEBUHR, PROTESTANT THEOLOGIAN

More organ music, quieter this time ...
A somber faced, ashen clergy approaches the pulpit. The congregation dutifully mirrors his expression. In a gloomy monotone, the mournful invitation is delivered: "Let Us Pray."

Apparently, there is a commandment out there that I missed; an eleventh one that must have broken off Moses's tablet:

11. *Thou shalt not show any emotion in prayer, most certainly not smiles, grins, or laughter.*

That, of course, is the adult version of the commandment. Kids like Ranger, however, would certainly have a different one. Theirs would read more like:

11. *Thou shalt not screen anything from God.*

It's not surprising. Kids are the freest of all God's creatures. They talk to anyone about anything. They ask questions when no one else would dream of it. They laugh when no one else would dare.

I was on the B train recently, heading to a meeting. It was rush hour, and the car was packed. No one spoke. No one made eye contact. But this was New York City. This is how it's done.

At least that's how it's done in the adult world. Somewhere around the 59th Street Station, a tiny little girl turned to an elderly, disheveled, somber-looking man sitting beside her and asked, "What is your name?"

Everyone in the car stared. This wasn't done. This just didn't happen.

"Sarah," her mom whispered, "don't bother the man."

"I'm Sarah," she continued, without giving her mom as much as a glance. "And this is Hop Hop," she said, holding up a ragged little rabbit missing one ear. "Did you know you have a hole in your jacket?"

"Yes," the man said, slowly looking around at the apprehensive faces in the subway train. "I tore it yesterday."

"How?" Sarah said expectantly.

He thought for a minute. Then smiled and asked, "How did Hop Hop lose his ear?"

At this point the entire train was entranced.

"It fell off in the washer," she said softly.

"Well, a rabbit ate my jacket!" he said with great gusto, pointing at Hop Hop. Sarah (and the entire train) began to laugh.

If only our conversations with God could be like that subway conversation. No screens, no fears, just honest, eager questions—and laughter at the end.

Unfortunately, many times our prayer lives parallel our love lives. We've all been there—that moment we first fall for someone and we just can't get enough. We want to hear all their stories, their jokes, their dreams. Then, after a time, we stop asking the questions. We lose interest. We stop listening.

It's the same with God. When we're young, we want to hear God's stories and jokes and dreams. Then, after a time, we stop asking the questions. We lose interest. We stop listening. We've heard it all before.

Without honesty or interest, there's no intimacy. Prayer becomes a dead ritual, like a conversation between a couple who long ago has stopped listening.

That's when a "subway" prayer comes in handy—a wide-eyed conversation full of interest and honest sharing—and laughter.

God understands all languages of our hearts. Think about the psalmist David, who danced and sang for God. Or the medieval sculptor Lorenzo Ghiberti, who prayed through gilt bronze. Consider Frida Kahlo, who called upon God through her vibrant, sensual paintings. Or Bach, who reached heavenward through the notes of his cantatas. Or Maya Angelou, who whispers her intimate prayer through poetry.

Let's boycott the eleventh commandment: *Thou shalt not show any emotion in prayer, most certainly not smiles, grins, or laughter.* Say what is in your heart. Ask honest questions. Listen for the response. Laugh when no one else would dare. Have a real live chat with God. Really ... how else can you have an honest conversation?

Get Out of the Living Room

> "To laugh often and much; to win the respect of intelligent people and the affection of children ... to leave the world a little better, whether by a healthy child, a garden patch or a redeemed social condition; to know even one life has breathed easier because you have lived. This is the meaning of success."
>
> —RALPH WALDO EMERSON, AMERICAN ESSAYIST AND POET

Still more majestic organ music ...

The prayer ends. A creed and the words of a well-worn hymn lull worshippers further into a vacant trance. Then the passing of the peace. People get out of their seats, voices engage, hugs and smiles are shared. There is a burst of life in the sanctuary. Then, as quickly as it began, it is snuffed out. All returns to silence.

I have come to the conclusion that all human gatherings break down into one of two categories: a living room gathering or a den gathering. This is true for board meetings, family dinners, relationships, or religious services. Unfortunately, most people treat houses of worship like a living room. Let me explain.

In my family home, as I was growing up, the living room was considered holy space. It was the place where all the "nice stuff" was kept: the chairs with my mom's handmade needle-point seats; the lamps with glass teardrop prisms dangling from under the shade; the stereo console that looked like a huge mahogany casket. We spoke of it (and *in* it) in hushed terms. There was never any laughter or loud voices heard in there. It was the kind of room that made you feel as if you should shower and put on a ball gown before you went in.

As a kid, my favorite room was not the living room, but the den. That's where all the fun was had. It was the room where Ginger, my brown, mixed-terrier mutt, was permitted. It was where I was allowed to make a fort out of the furniture. The den was where we would roast gooey, drippy marshmal-lows over an open fire; where loud, anxiety-filled Monopoly games were won and lost; where long naps were taken. The den was the room where life took place.

In most of our rituals and worship, we act as if we are sitting in the living room—the place with no life or warmth or energy. It's odd, if you think about it, given that most major religions worship a God who offers a message of joy and celebration.

We are perfectly capable of having fun and showing a festive spirit in other realms. Recently, I was watching the Tar Heels of the University of North Carolina play basketball against the evil empire of Duke University. We were cheering, then crying, then silent, then cheering all over again; all this over a one-time, two-hour event where the sole purpose is to place a small orange ball inside a suspended net. How ironic that in an ongoing, lifetime spiritual event concerned with the ultimate questions of existence, we sit silently, emoting nothing.

"What soap is to the body, laughter is to the soul."

—YIDDISH PROVERB

What would happen if we brought our spiritual rituals into the den where life takes place? Brought our worship into the place where messiness is allowed, where marshmallows are dripped and brown mixed-terrier mutts sleep? What would it be like to bring our whole selves, not just the somber, restrained adult, but our spontaneous, joyful seven-year-old as well? Whether it's a burp in the pulpit or laughter in prayer, God embraces our every cry—and every smile! It is only when we become as little children that our tears and our laughter will ring together in celebration of our faith.

REFLECTIONS

What age do you see yourself at heart? Why? Where is that little kid now? Is he or she welcomed in your life?

What made you laugh at that age? Do you still laugh at the same things? Do you allow yourself to?

Do you laugh in worship when you feel joy or experience humor? If not, why not? Who told you it was wrong?

How might your prayers change if you offered them like a five-year-old? Like the subway conversation? What words or emotions would be included that otherwise wouldn't have been offered?

Do you worship as if you are in the living room or the den? What would you like to change about that? Would you laugh more in the den?

8 Breathe, Just Breathe

The Healing Power of Breath and Laughter

Bursts of Laughter

"Mirth is God's medicine. Everybody ought to bathe in it."
— HENRY WARD BEECHER, NINETEENTH-CENTURY CLERGYMAN
AND REFORMER

Deep down, I wish I were Egyptian. I've always had a thing for desert landscapes. I often crave shawarma lamb wraps. And as a comedian, I am downright covetous of their ancient myths.

The ancient Egyptians offer some of the first known examples of laughter in religious realms, such as the myth of Adapa from the fifteenth century BCE. There, the God Anu is shown laughing at the mortal Adapa's attempt at eternal life.

Covet. Check.

Where I get seriously jealous, however, is with their creation myths. In our Abrahamic tradition, God *spoke* creation into being:

"Let there be light."

"Let dry land appear."

"Let the earth put forth vegetation."

While all fine and good, it does make God seem a bit bossy. I prefer the one offered by the ancient Egyptians where God *laughed* creation into being:

> When God laughed, seven gods were born to rule the world.... When he burst out laughing there was light.... When he burst out laughing the second time the waters were born; at the seventh burst of laughter, the soul was born.

Covet. Check, most definitely check.

Here was an entire civilization who believed that laughter is the source of all life. I love that image, especially when you consider what laughter is. Webster's defines the term *laugh* as "showing emotion with a chuckle or explosive vocal sound." In short, laughter is breath and energy. When you stop and think about it, it makes sense.

The moment we are born, we take our first breath. The moment we die, we exhale our last. And in between, in an average lifetime, we take some five hundred fifty million breaths. We can live for weeks without water and go months without food (although I'd prefer not to try). Without the intake of air, however, we are goners in a matter of minutes.

Breath drives all the major "life" functions. In fact, it operates similar to a trip to the grocery store. We go to the A & P and bring home a load of provisions (which for me is usually Ruffles and onion dip). We unpack the chips and dip, prepare it, and eat it. When done with the food, we haul the remaining trash to the street to be removed. Repeat.

Breathing is a similar routine. When we breathe in, we bring in a load of oxygen. Tiny capsules in our lungs send the oxygen into the bloodstream, which enables it to metabolize the Ruffles and onion dip into heat, energy, and life. Once the energy is burned, the oxygen turns into carbon dioxide and is then hauled back to the lungs to be removed when we exhale.

The more air we take in, the better the body functions. And one sure way to increase air intake is to laugh. When we laugh, we gulp in air, increasing our oxygen consumption and giving our diaphragm a good workout. Medical science has confirmed that the increased air through laughter can stimulate endorphins (nature's pain killers), boost immunity, ease digestion, improve mental functions, lower blood pressure, and increase overall wellness and healing. Obviously, the ancient Egyptians had this figured out long ago. Too bad it's only taken medical science three thousand five hundred years to catch up.

I always hate it when someone says, "Trust me." But in this case, *trust me*. I know firsthand about the psychological, physical, and spiritual healing power of breath and laughter. My experience began at 11:30 a.m. on June 2, 2007, at the NYU Medical Center.

Not a Good Sign

"He who laughs, lasts."

—MARY PETTIBONE POOLE, AUTHOR

"Is this going to take long?" I asked the nurse. I needed to know because I had wedged this terribly inconvenient medical test between two important meetings, and the time for the second was quickly approaching.

"I don't think so," she answered. The door then opened, and the doctor appeared with a pathologist in tow. Not a good sign.

"Ms. Sparks, I'm afraid the cells are cancerous," the doctor said in a flat monotone while looking at the report. "We will need to schedule surgery, then talk about radiation and chemo." They both gave me a look of "bummer" and quickly left the room.

I sat stunned with disbelief. A minute ago I was worried about a consulting gig for Goldman Sachs. Now, I had cancer?

After a few moments of silence, the well-meaning nurse turned to me and said, "Don't you worry, honey. The Lord will take care."

I'm sure I've said something similar to others in crisis, but right then it hit me wrong.

"Take *care?*" I snapped. "I think the Lord should have started a little earlier in taking care—like a couple of years ago when these cells started growing!"

She put her arm on my shoulder with this knowing look and said more forcefully, "Honey, *he* will take care."

I rolled my eyes.

"*He* has never had breast cancer, so I seriously doubt that *he* has any idea of how to 'take care' of this!"

The nurse shook her head in distain and walked out, leaving me alone with what were soon to become my two constant companions: cancer and sarcasm.

The Grief Trip

"Dread only one day at a time."
—CHARLIE BROWN

Most of us, unfortunately, are familiar with the stages of grief. Perhaps it's from a cancer diagnosis. Or maybe from the loss of a loved one, a job, or a marriage. Whatever the cause, grief is a slow path that has no shortcuts. There is, however, one secret: the better you feel, the easier the journey. And humor was the one thing that made me feel better.

STAGE 1: Denial

"Laughter is the sensation of feeling good all over and showing it principally in one place."
—JOSH BILLINGS, AMERICAN HUMORIST

For several weeks, denial, the first stage of grief, was my forte. In the beginning it was simply too much to comprehend that I was now one of "those people" who had cancer. I had read that one of the best ways to come to grips with denial is to share the news with other people. Bad plan.

"You have cancer? Wow. Does it hurt?"

"I'm so sorry. I'm sure you'll be fine."

"My best friend had breast cancer. I miss her so."

People can be so insensitive. The only alternative? Soften the blow through humor.

After a preliminary Google search on "cancer and humor," I found myself immersed in a number of sites dedicated to funny cancer products.

Within days, I was drinking my morning coffee out of a mug that said, "My oncologist can beat up your oncologist."

Then a new magnet appeared on my refrigerator: "Cancer—it's not just an astrological sign anymore."

At some point I bought a notepad that had a checklist at the top: "Buy milk, get gas, kick cancer's butt."

But my all-time favorite was a t-shirt with big red letters that said "Save the Titties."

Every time I saw that mug, magnet, or t-shirt, I started laughing. And you know what? I felt better.

At first I thought I felt better because I was simply using humor to block the shock and pain. But then I started doing some reading about humor and healing and discovered that laughter actually brings on a natural high in the body. In a study at Stanford University, researchers showed that laughing stimulates the parts of our brain that use dopamine, a kind of feel-good chemical messenger.

Fabulous! That meant that laughter falls into the category of two of my favorite things: chocolate and chili peppers. All three produce a major boost of endorphins, nature's own "happy pill": chili peppers through capsaicin, chocolate through serotonin, and laughter through the increased oxygen flow.

Medical studies have even shown that laughing produces the same level of mood-altering endorphins as a good workout. In fact, according to some studies, fifteen minutes of laughing can burn eighty calories, or a small chocolate brownie. Elliptical machine... or laughing? Not a hard call.

I felt better not because I was ignoring the pain, but because the humor took the edge off a little. It allowed me to turn directly into the ugly face of reality. Emily Dickinson wrote, "When giving me the truth, give it to me on the slant so I can bear it." Humor was the slant that allowed me to see the truth, hear it, and, ultimately, bear it.

STAGE 2: Anger

> "A clown is like an aspirin. Only he works twice as fast."
> —GROUCHO MARX, COMEDIAN AND FILM STAR

The second stage, anger, was a bit easier on me, but harder on the world. My new full-time job for at least the next six months was a series of tests and doctors and treatments. Like I had time for this? Like I wanted to be in the middle of this? Please.

The first week after my diagnosis, I was sent to get a CAT scan. In addition to being scared out of my wits, I was also in a surly mood, thanks to all the mountains of tests and appointments. After I arrived, the technician informed me that one of the tests he was going to perform was a liver scan. Allowing my anger to get the best of me, I said with a sigh, "Well, I had two beers last night. Just take that into consideration."

He looked at me with an exhausted glance, then left the room to administer the test.

After a few minutes, he returned with a grave look on his face. "We're not supposed to give test results on the spot." He paused, looked at the floor, and shook his head. "But you clearly have the early stages of what appears to be 'Bud Light' syndrome." Then he burst out laughing.

I stared at him in utter disbelief, then started laughing myself. As I walked home, I realized that I felt more relaxed and less angry.

"After you laugh, you go into a relaxed state," explains John Morreall, professor of religious studies at the College of William and Mary, in a *Psychology Today* article titled "Happily Ever Laughter." "Your blood pressure and heart rate drop below normal, so you feel profoundly relaxed."

Here was someone who faced down my angry words and surly energy with humor. Rather than mirror my emotion, he chose laughter. He changed the entire dynamic of our interaction. He changed me. And while I was still mad, the laughter slowly began to chip away at my prickly fortress of anger.

STAGE 3: Bargaining

"A good laugh and a long sleep are the best cures in the doctor's book."

—IRISH PROVERB

After the anger started to wane, I started to whine.

"Why me?"

"Why this?"

"Why now?"

It's easy to get consumed in the bargaining stage of grief, bogged down in the philosophical quicksand of "why?" trying to think of alternatives, ways around the difficulty. Maybe if I started eating macrobiotic health food, the tumor would simply go away. Or maybe if I took Chinese herbs, it would dissolve. Or perhaps I could workout so hard it would sweat its way out.

This is not a healthy stage. It is at this point that we all need a rope to pull us from its grip.

That's when my partner, Toby, offered to throw a party. A party? Seriously? I was getting ready to have surgery for breast cancer. And the reason to celebrate was *what*?

Slowly, I began to realize his wisdom. In the next few weeks, I found myself mentally pulling away from hospitals, doctors, and scary words such as "malignant." I also stopped thinking about health foods and Chinese herbs and elliptical machines.

I had to.

I had no time: We were busy airlifting pulled pork BBQ from the Pigman, one of my favorite places on the Outer Banks of North Carolina.

"Why me?" had been eclipsed by "Which one: vinegar or tomato sauce?" Rather than worrying about herbs or aerobics, I worried about whether we should serve potato salad or potato chips (we went with both); sweet tea or beer (we went with both); pecan pie or banana pudding (we went with, of course, both).

There is a power in altering your focus, even if for a minute, and making a choice to put something *else* in place of your fears and angst, especially if that priority is something fun.

Much of life's stress comes from feeling a loss of control. Choosing laughter and joy over worry helps us feel as if we have retaken control, even if in the smallest of spheres. Just giving myself permission to enjoy this party, and to temporarily thumb my nose at my looming sense of dread allowed me to recharge and re-engage treatment with renewed strength.

STAGE 4: Depression

> "A person without a sense of humor is like a wagon without springs. It's jolted by every pebble on the road."
>
> —HENRY WARD BEECHER, NINETEENTH-CENTURY
> CLERGYMAN AND REFORMER

Of course, there comes a point when we have exhausted all our abilities to deal with crisis. That's the point we sigh, hang our heads, and wait for life to plow us under.

That's when my congregation went to work. I began receiving a stream of funny e-mails and cards. One had a little piece of paper folded up in it that said, "I wanted to offer you a special prayer":

> Dear Lord, I want to thank you for taking such good care of me this day. With your help, I haven't known any fear or pain, I haven't felt depressed, and I haven't lost my temper or been impatient. But I am going to need extra help from you in a minute… because I'll be getting out of bed. Amen.

Then a lovely engraved card came from one of my senior and more "proper" members:

> I am thinking of you and hoping you might enjoy a smile over the following quote: "Eleanor Roosevelt once said: 'I had a rose named after me and I was very flattered. But I was not pleased to read the description in the catalog: No good in bed, but fine against a wall.'"

I felt almost immediately better, partly because my congregation had such an irreverent sense of humor, but also because the cards and jokes offered me a sense of solidarity.

The Comedy Cures Foundation is another place I experienced this feeling of solidarity. Founded by my friend Saranne Rothberg while battling stage IV cancer from her chemo chair, Comedy Cures offers therapeutic humor programs to kids and grown-ups living with illnesses and disabilities.

I was lucky enough to attend their "Laughing Lunch" held at the Broadway Comedy Club, where several comedians offered a show for a room full of patients and caregivers. At the end of the program, the woman next to me was in tears.

"Are you okay?" I asked.

"Yes," she said, smiling through the tears. "Now, I feel a little less alone."

In a *Psychology Today* article on "Happily Ever Laughter," Joseph Richman, professor emeritus at Albert Einstein Medical Center in the Bronx, New York, explains that laughter counteracts "feelings of alienation, a major factor in depression and suicide." Humor is about shared experiences and a feeling of belonging. It improves our mood through social connections. And when we feel less alone, we feel stronger.

STAGE 5: Acceptance

"A cheerful heart is good medicine."

—KING SOLOMON, PROVERBS 17:22

For me, the stages of grief were never predictable. One would never move seamlessly into another. One moment I would be in denial, then bargaining, then angry, then back to denial, then depressed; then I'd repeat all the steps all over again. I could never get a true read on where I was in the process.

I think the moment that I knew I had at least caught a glimmer of acceptance was on a motorcycle trip from Jackson Hole, Wyoming.* I had just finished my last radiation treatment and had flown directly to Wyoming to meet Toby, who had already ridden to Wyoming cross-country. As we were leaving Jackson together on the bike, we stopped for a photo in front of the Grand Teton range. It was that moment I looked at Toby and said, "There is our Christmas card ... this photo with the greeting: *Cancer can kiss our Tetons*."

---

*Yes, this was the infamous trip where we ended up at the Sea and Sand in Montana.

Over time, the consistent laughter helped me feel better and, in turn, helped me come to grips with the shock of the diagnosis a little faster. Whether cancer, the common cold, or just an annoying day, consistent laughter can boost our mood and make us feel better. And when we feel better, it can make life's journeys a little easier.

A Joke a Day Keeps the Co-Pays Away

"The art of medicine consists of keeping the patient amused, while nature heals the disease."

—VOLTAIRE, FRENCH PHILOSOPHER

The day of my surgery, I was a nervous wreck. Who wouldn't be? My blood pressure was through the roof, my heart rate was elevated, stress levels maxed.

As people were making the final preparations in the operating room, the anesthesiologist, seeing I was nervous, smiled at me, pointed at the IV, and said, "Don't worry, this stuff here? It's a *really* good year." I went under laughing—blood pressure a little lower, adrenaline and stress a bit less, muscles more relaxed. While a kind gesture, the anesthesiologist's humor may have played a more significant role in my recovery than just a simple joke.

It is no secret that laughing is an amazing healer. Back in 1979, *The New England Journal of Medicine* published a report based on Norman Cousins, a noted journalist and editor of the *Saturday Review*. In the 1960s Cousins had been diagnosed with a debilitating spinal disease and given a 1/500 chance of survival. Based on his belief in the importance of environment on healing, Cousins checked himself out of the hospital and into a hotel, where he took large doses of vitamin C and watched continual episodes of *Candid Camera* and the Marx Brothers. He found, over time, that laughter stimulated chemicals in his body that allowed him several hours of pain-free sleep. He continued the treatment until, eventually, his disease went into remission, and he was able to return to work. The study became the basis for a best-selling book, *Anatomy of an Illness,* as well as a television movie of the same name.

Since Cousins's ground-breaking study, numerous scientists and doctors have conducted similar tests with similar results. Some are enough to make you smile. The University of Maryland, for example, conducted a study where people were shown laughter-provoking movies to gauge their effect on cardiac health. The results, presented at the American College of Cardiology, showed that laughter appeared to cause the inner lining of blood vessels to dilate, thus increasing blood flow and avoiding dangerous vessel constriction. Consistent evidence has shown that laughter, over time, offers significant medical benefits, including boosting the immune system, lowering blood pressure, improving heart and respiratory functions, even regulating blood sugar.

This means that jokes pay off big time. Think of being in a room full of people where one person tells a joke, someone laughs, then another, then another … until contagious laughter fills the room. That's a little like the effect of laughter on the whole body. One deep belly laugh keeps growing till every part of the body is affected.

As Dr. Lee Berk, a professor at Loma Linda University's Schools of Medicine and Public Health put it in an article on humor therapy for Holisticonline.com, "If you took what we now know about the capability of laughter to manipulate the immune system, and bottled it, it would need FDA approval."

"Seven days without laughter makes one weak."

—MORT WALKER, CARTOONIST
AND CREATOR OF *BEETLE BAILEY*

Humor's effects on healing has grown so much that the field now has a long and fancy name: psychoneuroimmunology— the study of how psychological factors, the brain, and the immune system interact to influence health. Hospitals and treatment centers such as the Cancer Treatment Centers of America now employ humor therapy as part of their treatment options. The Chuckle Channel offered by the Health, Humor, and Hospitals Project provides in-hospital TV comedy programming for hospitals and treatment centers across the county. And the Big Apple Circus has a pediatric clown care unit that is dedicated to bringing laughter and joy to hospitalized children.

Four years after my diagnosis, I am cancer free. I am thankful for the medical care I received; but most of all I am thankful for the joyful attitude of the doctors, nurses, and caregivers with whom I was privileged to work. While the surgery and radiation certainly had a part, I am convinced that the encouragement I received to laugh was the most powerful treatment of all.

Perhaps my story is your story, too. Many of us have faced places of physical pain or illness. Many of us have lived the long, unpredictable stages of grief. We've all been there in some form, and we've all searched for some healing and comfort.

"The human race has only one effective weapon and that
   is laughter."

—MARK TWAIN

Breath and laughter are the most healing of forces. Physically, they strengthen and fortify out bodies. Spiritually, they bolster our souls. The Hebrew word for breath, *ruach,* is also the same word for spirit. As we laugh, we breathe in air *and* spirit. You might even say as we laugh we inhale the power of God.

The Egyptians were right. Breath and laughter *are* the source of all life.

Covet. Check. Most definitely, check.

REFLECTIONS

What makes you laugh out loud? If you don't know, listen to yourself for the next few days and make a list of what makes you laugh.

The Bible is composed of a collection of books, or a canon. That is a holy canon. How about building yourself a humor canon? Think about making a collection of videos, books, cartoons, sounds, images, letters that make you smile or laugh. Can you imagine how these might aid your physical, mental, and spiritual healing?

9 Into the Ark
Laughter in Times of Crisis

The Lifeboat of Laughter

"An endless rain is just beginning. Into the ark, for where
else can you go."

—WISLAWA SZYMBORSKA, NOBEL LAUREATE POET

Humor and arks are two things you wouldn't normally put
together. Of course, most people wouldn't put humor and religion together either. Thank goodness for Bill Cosby who
brought together all three.

In his famous 1963 stand-up routine on Noah, Cosby
talked about the difficulties of loading an ark:

Noah had a heck of a job. He had to go out and collect
the animals in the world by twos, two mosquitoes …
male and female. And he had to keep telling the rabbits
only two, *only* two, *only* two!

And, of course, then there was the conversation between God
and Noah regarding the ark:

Very few people know about the conversation between
Noah and the Lord …

"Noah?"

"Who is that?"

"It's the Lord."

"Right!"

"I want you to build an ark."

"Right! [long pause] What's an ark?"

"Go get some wood and build it 300 cubits by 80 cubits by 40 cubits."

"Right! [long pause] What's a cubit?"

"Let's see ... I used to remember ..."

With this routine, Cosby not only blazed a new path by bringing religion into stand-up, he also tapped a deeper link, for both arks and humor offer refuge in times of crisis.

"If you find yourself going through hell, keep going."

—WALT DISNEY

For thousands of years, arks have been an archetype of protection and safety. The book of Genesis tells the story of six-hundred-year-old Noah building a wooden boat and saving creation from God's great flood. But Genesis isn't the only place we find this story.

The Hopi Indians tell a story where the people were warned of a great flood and told to crawl into the hollow stems of giant reeds that surrounded their village. The gods then caused a great flood, and the people floated atop the flood waters, and the reeds carried them to safety.

The Aborigines in Australia tell a story of a frog who swallowed all the water in the world and caused a great drought. The only way to stop the drought was to make the frog laugh. Animals from all over the world came to make him laugh. Finally, the eel made the frog laugh and water poured from his mouth and a great flood came. Then the pelican went from island to island rescuing people in a great canoe.

While we typically expect arks to come in the form of large wooden boats, humor is another, less literal type of ark that also offers refuge.

On September 12, 2001, I was working for the Red Cross in downtown Manhattan. We were taking inbound calls for missing persons in the fallen World Trade Center Towers. About halfway through the shift, my phone rang and a woman's voice tentatively said, "I need your help."

Slowly, she began offering a missing person's report for her husband who had been working on one of the higher floors of the south tower. She described him in great detail: where he worked, what he looked like, how the rescue workers might recognize him. Suddenly, in the middle of her description, she began to laugh hysterically.

"Oh, I forgot to tell you," she blurted out. "He left the house with the *worst* tie on! It was like this horrible green color with flamingos and palm trees." She continued to laugh.

Unsure of how to respond, I said nothing.

Eventually, she stopped laughing.

After a moment of silence, she said, "You must think me crazy laughing like this." She paused again, then whispered, "But laughter is *all* my family and I have left."

An ark in a different form, laughter can act as a lifeboat for those in crisis: a place of protection, a means of moving to and through grief, a vessel that can carry us above the pain, a second chance.

Precious Cargo

"Laughter is God's soothing touch on a fevered world."
—KENNETH HILDEBRAND, AUTHOR

One of the more foolish things I have done in my life is to watch the movie *Titanic* for the first time the night before I took a cruise to the Bahamas. Granted, there were no reports of large icebergs off the coast of Miami, but, nonetheless, I *knew* there was some lurking danger in those icy Caribbean waters. As we pulled away from the cruise ship terminal, I waved my final goodbyes—a last act, I was sure, before an inevitable watery death.

Good thing Noah was a bit nervier. He loaded his entire family and most of creation onto a wooden ship; nothing between his precious cargo and the raging flood waters but a tiny hull made of gopher wood.

Of course, Noah was not the only one who knows about raging flood waters. We all have faced flood waters in life, whether through loss or pain or illness. And, like Noah, we too carry a precious cargo inside—the cargo of spirit.

In times of crisis, our spirit can be threatened or damaged. Worse, the crisis can start to define us, taking over what used to be our life force and soul.

Humor offers us our own gopher-wood hull that can protect us in the floods of life. When we can laugh in a place of pain, we are reminded of our capacity to feel joy amid suffering. We can remember who we are.

One group that harnesses such a power is Clowns without Borders. Following the logo, "No Child without a Smile," the group uses laughter and clowning to relieve the suffering of children who live in areas of crisis. Sponsoring projects such as a circus in a Palestinian refugee camp and therapeutic humor residencies for kids with AIDS in South Africa, Clowns without Borders gives children a way to protect their own precious cargo: their childhood.

"In a lot of these places, children can't be kids. It's a luxury to live a childhood," shared a group member. "They have food, they have housing. But they also need to experience their humanity, and that is what we bring."

Moshe Cohen, founder of the American branch of Clowns without Borders, tells a story of doing therapeutic work with children in Kosovo, a country that had been destroyed during the ethnic conflict. Cohen invited these kids to pretend to be wolves howling at the moon.

"All of a sudden, I saw all these adult faces popping over the wall to see what was happening. Everyone started laughing."

Suffering is not who we *are;* it is what we are *experiencing.* Laughter is what can protect us from being defined by our pain. It holds our spirits safe while we sail treacherous waters. It's our own personal version of a gopher-wood hull, reassuring us that no matter what comes at us, even if it defeats us, it will never define us.

Tears of Laughter

"I always knew looking back on my tears would bring me laughter, but I never knew looking back on my laughter would make me cry."

—CAT STEVENS, BRITISH SINGER-SONGWRITER

It was my first funeral as newly ordained clergy. The service was being held an hour and a half from my church on the far end of Staten Island. It was pouring rain. Three strikes!

The funeral was for Mary, the ninety-five-year-old matriarch of a large family in my congregation. A beautiful woman full of life and passion, Mary always took pride in her appearance.

When I arrived at the funeral home, I was escorted by Mary's daughter, Nancy, over to the casket to say a prayer. As we bowed our heads, I placed one hand on Nancy's shoulder, and with the other I reached into the casket. When I touched Mary's arm, I froze. It was hard with sharp edges—almost square.

"*What* is this?" I blurted out, pulling my hand out of the casket. (Probably not the most pastoral of responses.)

Nancy opened her eyes, looked down at Mary, and then broke out laughing.

"Oh, I forgot," she said pulling out a box from within Mary's sleeve. "We slipped in a bottle of Miss Clairol hair color for Mama's journey. She always worried that they might not have her exact formula on the other side."

We laughed until we cried, and then cried until we started laughing again. That was our prayer.

Tears of laughter and tears of mourning are virtually the same. The unfortunate difference is that we learn to share our tears of joy and hide our tears of sorrow. To do so makes us feel strong, as if we are somehow beyond the pain and grieving.

Unfortunately, sometimes we get stuck in this place of no tears, a place where we don't even remember how to grieve. Humor can help break this block. Like Noah's ark, humor can transport us from one point to another: from laughter to tears, and tears back to laughter.

In the weeks following 9/11, when all late-night comedians were quiet, the stand-up comedian Reno bravely opened a comedy show off-Broadway. The show, "Rebel without a Pause," was framed around her experiences on the morning of 9/11. An instant hit, her comedy provided a safe space for the audiences to simultaneously share their grief and laugh at their common experiences.

Noting the designer luggage carried by her escaping Tribeca neighbors and their clear status as "first-time runners," Reno dubbed her community "nouvelle refugees from Tribecastan." She went on to inquire, "Where was the emergency broadcast system that day?" and "Why was the National Guard wearing *jungle* camouflage in Manhattan?"

Her material walked the audience—many of whom had lost loved ones in the attack—through the trauma of 9/11, evoking laughter, then tears, then more laughter, and finally, hope.

Kahlil Gibran wrote, "The self-same well from which your laughter rises was often times filled with your tears." Tears of sorrow and tears of laughter come from the same place. And because of that, sometimes only laughter can help us access those deep places of pain.

Rising Above the Flood

"In times like these, it is helpful to remember that there have always been times like these."

—PAUL HARVEY, AMERICAN RADIO BROADCASTER

One of two things can happen to an ark when flood waters hit: it can sink or it can float. Thank goodness, Noah nailed that ark pretty tight: *"The flood continued forty days on the earth; and the waters increased, and bore up the ark, and it rose high above the earth"* (Genesis 7:17). Not only did the ark hold, it rose above the raging waters and ultimately carried Noah to safety.

In any crisis, we face the same ark options: we can allow ourselves to sink, drowning in a sea of self-pity, blame, or despair, dragging everyone down into the flood waters with us; or we can bear ourselves up and float above the pain, bringing up those around us as well. As Rev. Calvin Butts, pastor of the Abyssian Baptist Church, said, "The will of God is never seen in tragedies. The will of God is seen in our response to tragedy."

My dad died a few years ago at the ripe old age of eighty-nine. Before he passed, he spent a long time in the hospital, quite sick and in a lot of pain. One day when I was sitting with him in hospice, a new nurse came into the room. She looked suspiciously like a Dallas Cowboy cheerleader.

"Mr. Sparks?" she cooed.

My dad opened one eye, then both, and upon getting a clear view of his new nurse, began to sit up a bit and straighten his pajamas. A miracle, I thought to myself.

"I'm here to check your catheter," said the cheerleader.

Faster than I had moved in years, I got up to excuse myself from the room. But before I even made it to the door, Dad took a deep breath and in his thick Southern accent said, "Well, honey, you just make yourself *to home!*"

At that point in his life, my dad could have easily chosen to be surly and difficult. No one would have blamed him. But he chose a different tact. He chose joy. And in that moment of laughter, he not only rose above the pain, but he brought joy and lightness to all around him as well.

Humor is the ark that will allow us to rise above. It is God's way of lifting our burdens, if just for a split second, to allow us a moment to breathe and to heal.

A means of transcendence, humor empowers us to let go of the things that weigh us down, such as anger and blame, and frees us to rise above. Perhaps Bill Cosby put it best when he said, "You can turn painful situations around through laughter. If you can find humor in anything, even poverty, you can survive it."

Humor as a Second Chance

"Some who cannot say a prayer may still be able to dance it. People who cannot hope may be able to laugh."
—HARVEY COX, PROFESSOR, HARVARD DIVINITY SCHOOL

In early 2005, I took a trip to Death Valley. Clearly, this is not everyone's first choice of vacation spots. But at this particular time and at this particular place, it was mine.

A miracle was happening in the California desert. The previous winter had brought the area a few more inches of rain than normal, and in February, its otherwise bleak sand dunes and rocks were covered with tiny wildflowers. Desert gold, blazing star, poppies, verbenas, and evening primrose blanketed the landscape. I immediately bought a ticket and flew there to see this phenomenon: a place of hope and renewal, life from no life; a second chance.

As I walked through those desert blooms, I was reminded of Noah and how he must have felt when the rain stopped and the mountain tops appeared and the dove he sent to search for land returned with an olive branch. Finally ... at last ... life.

In every crisis and every place of pain, there comes a second chance, a place where we can reclaim our spirit and our power. And like the flowers in Death Valley, that point is usually marked by some tiny sign of life breaking through: a smile, a laugh, a small signal of resurrection. When we find something to smile about in a place of pain, the balance of power shifts and we reclaim control. We take life back.

Ed Bradley of CBS's *60 Minutes,* an avid jazz aficionado, died at age sixty-five from leukemia. His funeral included a New Orleans funeral brass band and performances by Jimmy Buffet, Aaron Neville, and Wynton Marsalis. In planning the music, it is said that Bradley offered the following instructions: "You can make the first line as slow and sad as you want, but in the second line, you better bring a little tambourine."

There are times in life when we face insurmountable obstacles: cancer, a divorce, the loss of a loved one, depression, financial difficulty, or losing a job. Times when life appears at an end, when we feel like giving up, calling it a day, phoning it in. But in every crisis and every place of pain, there comes a second chance, a place where we can "bring a little tambourine." And humor is what can empower us to take that step.

The philosopher Albert Camus once said, "In the depths of winter, I finally learned that within me there lay an invincible summer." We all have that gift of an invincible summer within; a holy gift where we realize that there is delight in the simple drawing of a breath, no matter what the circumstances.

When we face the raging flood waters, when we find ourselves in the shadow of a looming storm cloud, we need to remember Nobel Laureate poet Wislawa Szymborska's words: "An endless rain is just beginning. Into the ark, for where else can you go."

REFLECTIONS

Think of the times when you have found yourself in need of an emotional or spiritual ark. What became your ark? What lifted your spirits? Did it include any lightness or laughter?

Have you ever laughed when you couldn't cry? What happened? Did the tears eventually come? How did you feel after the release?

What second chances do you need in your life? How might cultivating a sense of humor help you get there? Where could you look for places and people who could help you smile more?

10 A Leo's Search for God

Laughter Helps Us Keep Faith When God Is Silent

God Is a Scorpio

> "God is silent. Now if only man would shut up."
> —WOODY ALLEN, COMEDIAN, WRITER, AND DIRECTOR

I am a spiritual seeker and a Leo. As such, I prefer chatty, outgoing deities. I want a God who wants to talk about the same things I do—that is, me; a God who tells me when I wake up each morning that I look gorgeous; a God who says, "I love you," every five seconds, and, "You are so fabulous," every ten.

I didn't ask to be born in August. I didn't even ask to be a Leo. But since someone or something *chose* to put me on this earth during that particular planetary grade, one would *think* that he, she, or it would take the time to ensure that my royal Leo requirements were met. Unfortunately, the deity responsible was, I believe, a Scorpio: a private, quiet sign that hates lengthy conversations.

I first noticed this astrological breakdown at an early age. People on television, usually men with puffy, white, blow-dried hair, would say that God had told them thus and such, and therefore we should do this and that. Why didn't God just talk to me directly? I, too, had questions. But unlike the television chosen, I never seemed to get any answers.

Maybe it was because I lived in the South and my accent was too heavy for God to understand.

Or perhaps it was the weather. Down South, summer, which ran early February through late November, was always hot and humid. Perhaps the number of answered prayers simply went down a good part of the year because, like every other Southerner in the heat, God simply felt sluggish or a bit short tempered.

Or maybe it was because God simply had too many prayers to answer. I knew there were six billion people inhabiting the earth. If half were asleep at any given time, and only 10 percent of the three billion who were awake felt like praying, that's still millions of people praying. And that's just *people*. What if animals prayed, too? And plants? And rocks? And what about life in other galaxies? And, of course, let's not forget the angels and archangels who pray loudly and all the time. God has a lot to listen to.

Alas, none of those excuses made me feel any better. The only thing that did make me feel better was something I learned later in life: My struggle was not limited to Leos.

You don't have to be a fiery lioness to feel the weight of holy silence. We've all had that moment when we look around expectantly for some divine response—any response—and there appears to be none. Why does God sometimes appear silent? And why do those times seem to be when we most need holy assistance?

Of course, over time I also learned that Leos never believe anything is their fault. Which then made me wonder, was the problem really with God?

We Don't Know

"We are an advanced breed of monkey on a tiny unremarkable planet revolving around a below average star."
—STEPHEN HAWKING, BRITISH PHYSICIST

English is one of the more difficult languages to learn. And within that language, there is a three-word phrase that most people find impossible to master: "I don't know." We'd rather speculate, gesticulate, obfuscate—*anything*—rather than just admit the honest truth that we don't know.

Just because we sent a little robot to Mars and rolled it around the surface, we believe that we have cracked the code on all of life's great mysteries. Reality check: We may be able to clone a sheep, but we still can't cure the common cold.

It is human nature to want to believe that we know everything. The alternative—the unknown—is simply too scary. This is especially true when it comes to God.

We paint and carve elaborate images we believe represent God. We pontificate on "who God likes and does not like." We especially love to talk with authority about how and when God speaks and why God is sometimes silent. *But we don't know*.

Many of us were programmed at an early age to expect God to "speak" in very limited and scheduled ways. In my case, it was Sundays at 11 a.m. in a Baptist church. If you didn't go to that Baptist church on that Sunday at that time, you were going to miss the one broadcast you would get for the week. It was as if each service ended with, "This concludes God's message. God has left the building. God will return next Sunday, same time, same place." It never dawned on me that there might be additional broadcasts.

Given the limited holy frequencies to which we listen, we probably miss 99 percent of God's broadcasts. How could we think that God speaks in only one way? If Gatorade and Snapple see the need for marketing variety, surely God does as well.

As we get older, we think we get more sophisticated in our understanding of God. We think we know more about God and have a grasp on why God does or does not do certain things. *But we don't know.* And, in fact, we haven't known for a long, long time.

A few thousand years ago there lived a man the Hebrew Bible calls Job. As the story goes, Job hit some hard times and blamed God. He blamed God because, of course, Job knew *everything*, including the part about God being responsible for all of Job's pain. For thirty-seven verses, during which God was silent, Job whined, "*Why* did you do this to *me*?"

Finally, in chapter 38, God had had enough and began to speak:

> "*Who* is this running their mouth without anything to back it up? Man-up, Job. If you know so much about me and the workings of the universe, tell me, where were you when I laid the foundations of the earth? I didn't see you there at the time.
>
> [pause, expectant look]
>
> "Who was responsible for the measurements?
>
> "Who laid the cornerstone?

"Who fastened the foundations?
[cynical look forms, folding of holy arms]
"Come on, Job, I *know* you know.
"Okay. Let's try something easier …
"How do you make it rain in the desert?
"How do you make grass grow?
"What is the location of my storehouses of snow
and hail?
"Where do I keep the keys to the gates of hell?
[pause, smug smile]
"Please, Job, tell me. I'm all ears."*

I have always thought that God sounded a bit like Joan Rivers in this story. Too bad Job didn't have the same sense of humor. The ability to laugh might have saved him an awful lot of angst. Like most of us, he just didn't realize that laughter can help us let go of our human desire for control and our constant need for answers.

Let Go and Laugh

"One doesn't have a sense of humor. It has you."
—LARRY GELBART, AWARD-WINNING
COMEDY WRITER AND CREATOR OF *MASH*

One of my summer jobs in high school was at Carowinds theme park selling tacky gifts, like glow-in-the-dark jewelry and blown-glass swans. It was a great job. Great, that is, until I almost got fired.

---

*Taken from the NRSV (New Reverend Susan Version).

One sultry summer night, I was assigned to work the Palladium amphitheater where the comedian Steve Martin was performing. My mission? To walk through the crowd selling the ubiquitous Steve Martin arrow-through-the-head hats. I was doing a fine job until he came on and started his King Tut routine.

Halfway down aisle seven, I heard the refrain: "Born in Arizona, moved to Babylonia, King Tut … funky Tut." That was it. I started laughing and couldn't stop.

"He coulda won a Grammy, buried in his Jammies. He was born in Arizona, got a condo made of stone-a, King Tut!"

The next thing I know, I was sitting next to a total stranger, doubled over, crying, the arrow hats on the ground. I couldn't move until the song finally stopped. While my sales that night were a point of contention with my boss, I learned a good lesson about the involuntary nature of humor.

> "You can't deny laughter; when it comes, it plops down in your favorite chair and stays as long as it wants."
>
> —Stephen King, author

At some point, we have all been hit with that bout of uncontrollable laughter, the kind where you are gasping for breath, holding your side, tears streaming down your face. Some people call it "helpless with laughter." The *Encyclopedia Britannica* calls it a "rhythmic, vocalized, expiratory, involuntary action." I prefer the "helpless with laughter" description, as the other sounds more like a death scene from *Hamlet*. Whatever the description, laughter is the ultimate sign of letting go of control.

At its most basic, laughter is an involuntary reaction to the difference between what we expect and what we see. We laugh, for example, at the proud person slipping on the ice, based on the contrast of his or her dignity and the undignified plight. Sure, we may try to hold our breath to control the reaction, but nine out of ten times, it doesn't work.

"Laughter isn't under our conscious control," explains Robert Provine, professor of psychology and neuroscience at the University of Maryland in a WebMD article on "Why We Laugh." "We don't choose to laugh in the same way that we choose to speak ... laughter can't always be tamed."

Laughter is not only an involuntary action of the body, it can also be a sign of the mind letting go. And I don't mean a *One Flew Over the Cuckoo's Nest* kind of letting go. I'm speaking of an intellectual and spiritual release.

Buddhism, for example, teaches that to move toward enlightenment, we must let go of the rational mind and its need for rational answers. Zen Buddhists see laughter as a tool that enables enlightenment as it deflates ego and pride, and mocks our attempts at control.

Rather than making students read this only in a book, Buddhist teachers use paradoxical statements, or koans, to demonstrate the point. Meant to frustrate and confuse, the meaning of a particular koan cannot be accessed through reason or rational thinking.

"What is the sound of one hand clapping?"

"Has a dog Buddha-nature or not?"

"What is the sound of a tree falling in the forest, if there is no one there to hear it?" (Of course there is the twenty-first-century Western counterpart: "If a man says something in a forest and there is no woman around to hear, is he still wrong?")

The student is left only with the ability to laugh at the mind's futile attempt to control and reason. Bottom line? *We don't know.*

Laughter has also shown itself to be a sign of spiritual surrender. As early as the sixth century, we see the "Holy Fool" tradition beginning to emerge. Based on Paul's teaching in 1 Corinthians 4:10, "We are fools for Christ's sake," a type of sainthood developed where piety was shown through making a fool of yourself.

There was Andrew the Fool in the seventh century, who lived a life of feigned madness and spent much of his time naked, homeless, and sleeping on a dung heap. In Russia, Basil the Blessed dedicated himself to justice and the plight of the poor, offering a plate of raw meat to Ivan the Terrible as a statement against Ivan's murderous politics.

More recently, the charismatic Christian movement has followed suit. Worshippers in the "Holy Laughter Movement" break into uncontrollable laughter, dancing and rolling in the aisles. The founder and pastor Rodney Howard-Browne calls himself "the Holy Ghost bartender," as his congregation is drunk with joy. Some members are so full of the spirit, they feel physically unable to get up, stuck in what they call "Holy Ghost glue."

Whether with a Zen monk, a medieval Holy Fool, or a Holy Ghost bartender, laughter is simply another version of throwing up your hands and saying, "I give up!" We laugh in order to say, "We don't know." And not knowing is ultimately okay.

Of course, there is always that lurking outside possibility that there are no answers; that, perhaps, the universe is one great practical joke. The author John Lloyd offers an interesting perspective. In the Bible, the book of John begins, "In the beginning was the Word and the Word was with God and the Word was God" (1:1). *Word,* in this context, is translated from the Greek *logos,* traditionally defined as "word" or "thought."

However, Lloyd points out that in Latin, *logos* may also be defined as "joke." This definitely puts a different spin on the Gospel: "In the beginning was the Joke and the Joke was with God and the Joke was God."

If we can get past our knee-jerk "this-is-blasphemy!" reaction, perhaps we can find in this twist of translation a new paradigm, a recognition that perhaps in life there are no answers, that creation is beyond explanations and control. So we can laugh and let go. And in this place where all is released, all becomes possible.

When All Is Gone, All Is Possible

> "At the height of laughter, the universe is flung into a kaleidoscope of new possibilities."
> —JEAN HOUSTON, AMERICAN AUTHOR AND SPIRITUAL LEADER

One thing I have learned over the years about Scorpios is that they are loyal beyond imagination. Often found in the background, they are, nonetheless, always there—a bit like Forest Gump. In the movie, Forest magically materializes out of the background in some of the major historical moments of the time. Oh, there was Forest with President John F. Kennedy! Oh, there he was with Elvis Presley! Oh, look, there was Forest standing beside John Lennon! You had to look closely to see him, but he was always there, not so unlike a Scorpio God.

The ancient Celts apparently agreed with my assessment that God was a Scorpio. In Celtic spirituality, in order to find God, you have to look pretty hard. But if you look in the right places, God is always there.

One of those places is what the Celts deemed "thin places," places where the boundary between human and holy is so thin, so transparent, you can almost break through. These are the places where secular and holy, earth and heaven, ordinary and sacred come together. As the theologian Marcus Borg explains, "Thin places are places where the veil momentarily lifts, and we behold God."

Thin places can take many forms. Some are geographical, like the desert, for example, where all things are stripped away and life is down to its bare essentials. Others might be found in music, poetry, literature, or art. Sometimes even people can offer a thin place, a point where we are able to encounter the holy.

Another thin place we don't often think of is laughter. It clears our hearts of insecurity, neediness, and stale expectations. It opens our hearts anew for the words or songs or silence we were meant to receive. With laughter, our hearts are laid bare before God.

In a way, it's like cleaning out a closet. In my closet, for example, there are clothes that date from the disco era. I'm not proud of it, but there it is. The six-foot-by-two-foot space is crowded beyond imagination, due to sparkly tube tops, cowl-neck satin appliqué sweaters, and white denim stirrup pants tucked in the back. I don't wear them. I don't even like them. But I have a hard time getting rid of them. Unfortunately, it makes for little room for more modern, relevant clothes.

Similarly, an honest spiritual search requires us to let go of our expectations, our need for answers. As author Anne Lamott said, "God can't clean the house of you with you still in it."

Of course, the irony of all this is hard to miss. We get mad because God seems silent. So we laugh and shrug and finally admit we don't have answers. And in that moment of giving up our need for answers, suddenly we can hear God again.

It's a familiar quandary. Like my relationship with my keys. Most mornings I go stomping through the house yelling, "*Who* took my keys!" Finally, I sigh, give up, and sit down. And, miraculously, there they are in front of me, sitting on the kitchen table.

> "When God speaks, it is a good idea to listen. When some-
> one else tells you God spoke, best double check."
>
> —DICK ROGERS, EDITOR

After much angst and hand-wringing and throwing rocks at the sky, I have come to the conclusion that God is silent through no fault of God. The Trappist monk Thomas Merton said, "Life is this simple. We are living in a world that is absolutely transparent, and God is shining through it all the time. This is not just a fable or a nice story. It is true. [And] if we abandon ourselves to God and forget ourselves, we see it sometimes."

In the end, I still see myself as a Leo with a Scorpio Creator. But through laughter, I've found a thin place where even Leos and Scorpios are compatible, a point where we let go and stop trying to make God into something; a place of repose where, resting in the mystery, we simply await God to reveal God's self in God's own time. No expectations. No disappointments. Just faith that what comes is holy and right and meant to be … Scorpio, Leo, or whatever.

REFLECTIONS

What is your experience of infectious smiles? Have you ever watched a smile "travel" around a room of people? How have you seen such a smile change people?

Have there been times in your life when you have felt that God was silent? Could you have missed the broadcast? Do you have specific expectations of how God should sound? When or where should God show up?

What are your "thin places," places or times when you feel closer to God, spaces where the veil between human and holy is thin? Is laughter a part of this place?

Think of a time when you were helpless with laughter. Have you ever considered incorporating such laughter in your spiritual journey? Using it as a sign of spiritual surrender? Letting go in front of God?

11 The Dash In Between

How We Live and What We Leave

The Critical Part of the Formula

"It is not our abilities that show who we are, but our choices."

—DUMBLEDORE, TO HARRY POTTER

When we die (you *know* a chapter is going to be good when it starts like that ...), there will be three things on our tombstone, two of which are utterly useless. The first is our birth date. That number is good for soliciting presents. Period. And, frankly, after a certain point in life, even presents can't make up for the depressing nature of birthdays.

The second thing is the date we died. Unlike birthdays, that number offers no option for presents. In fact, it has no relevance in the great scheme of things. None of us know it in advance. Yet most of us spend our entire lives worrying about when it will happen. The irony is that the more we worry about the second date, the less we actually focus on the third thing on the tombstone—*and* the most critical part of the formula: the dash in between.[*]

It is not when we are born. It is not when we die. It is the time lived in between that truly matters.

How's It Going?

> "Life is too important to be taken seriously."
>
> —OSCAR WILDE, LATE-NINETEENTH-CENTURY PLAYWRIGHT

So, how *is* that "dash in between" going? Without thinking, most people will offer the standard knee-jerk reaction: "Fine. It's just fine."

"How are you?"

"Fine."

"How's the job?"

"Fine."

"How's the family?"

"Fine."

"How are you feeling about the fact that the second date on your tombstone is quickly approaching and that your life to date may be a royal mess?"

"Fine. Just fine."

These days, we don't like to go deep. Or think too hard. Or ask too many questions. We roll our eyes at what we deem flimsy New Age pursuits, such as looking at our life and asking if we have lived how we wanted. We anesthetize ourselves into offering the pat response "fine." Offering it and, worse, believing it.

---

[*]The idea of life as a "dash in between" was inspired by a poem called "The Dash" by Linda Ellis.

It's hard to face the fact that the dash in between is flying past, that we may already be a third of the way through, or a half, or almost done. It's doubly hard to come to terms with the fact that our life lived to date *may not* be what we intended. So we smile, and nod, and say with a forced smile, "It's fine. Just fine."

"How's it going?" is not a hard or time-consuming question to answer. It does not require us to fill multiple journals, or chant while holding a painful pretzel-like pose, or retreat to a remote Himalayan cave.

And it's not like we don't have time to think about it. Recently, I saw a study on how people use their time. The results were startling. Over an average lifespan, we spend:

- Five years on the Internet
- Eleven years in front of television
- Twenty-six years sleeping and
- Twenty weeks on hold

This last entry was especially troubling. Twenty weeks listening to Muzak? *Five months* of Lionel Richie and Yani? Surely we could find something better to do with our lives. All we have to do is just look at one day, perhaps even one moment of one day, and ask ourselves, "How did I spend my time?"

> "Laughter is carbonated holiness."
>
> —ANNE LAMOTT, AUTHOR

Granted, every day is different, and certainly some days are better than others. But in general, we tend to hold to the same simple patterns of behavior.

The late Carnegie Mellon professor Randy Pausch delivered a lecture to his students after he was diagnosed with terminal pancreatic cancer. Using an analogy from *Winnie the Pooh,* he argued that, in life, people have two simple choices: Be an Eeyore or a Tigger. These two furry characters sum up the spectrum of human behavior.

Eeyore is the pessimistic, whiny donkey who plods around with his head down, looking forlorn. Always negative, he has low expectations for himself and others, and doesn't think he does anything right.

On the opposite end of the spectrum is the eager, exuberant Tigger, who goes bouncing through life on his tail. Tigger looks for joy, no matter what the circumstances.

Call it what you will: glass half-empty versus glass half-full, or optimist versus pessimist. Bottom line, in any given circumstances, we have two choices: We can laugh or we can cry.

Studies say that, on average, a person laughs six minutes a day, but complains for eight. I realize that, at best, these are rough, random statistics that don't speak for every individual. However, for many of us they may be sadly accurate. If we took one day in time and looked at our behavior, I am afraid many of us would have an inordinately long column for Eeyore and a relatively short one for Tigger.

So, how's it going so far? Do you spend more time laughing or complaining? As Eeyore or Tigger? Think hard about it, for it matters more than you may think.

Change the World One Smile at a Time

"That which dominates our imaginations and our thoughts will determine our life and our character. Therefore, it behooves us to be careful what we worship, for what we are worshipping we are becoming."

—RALPH WALDO EMERSON, AMERICAN ESSAYIST AND POET

When it comes to first words, most kids start with the basics, like *mama* or *dada*. My first word, however, was *pancake*. Pancakes were my first great love (bordering on obsession). And not just any pancakes, but chocolate pancakes, the kind where you drop chocolate chips into the batter as it's cooking so they melt and get gooey and sticky.

As a toddler, I would take these chocolate treasures from the breakfast table and carry them throughout the house, nibbling as I went. They became a part of me—literally: me, my face, my hands. You could always tell where I'd been in our house by the little chocolate handprints. They made quite a lasting impression.

The same holds true in life. What we carry with us becomes who we are. And we should choose carefully. Like those pancakes, whatever we carry makes an impact on everything we touch. Even the smallest handprints can make a lasting impression. And nowhere is this more evident than in the simple act of a smile.

> "The spiritual person isn't the one in the white robe, it's the one who smiles back."
>
> —HEATHER KING, AUTHOR AND RADIO COMMENTATOR

Scientists and psychologists as far back as Charles Darwin and William James have argued that emotions can be regulated by behavior, particularly by facial expressions. The modern theory, known as the "facial feedback hypothesis," offers compelling evidence that smiling leads to physiological changes in the brain that cool the blood, which in turn controls our mood, causing a feeling of happiness. In short, we can change our inward emotion by changing our outward expression. Said another way, "Fake it till you make it."

What we feel in our hearts manifests itself in our behavior. And how we act over time is what we become. Consistently reminding ourselves to form a smile throughout our daily lives may over time change our hearts. And when our hearts change, the way we encounter the world changes. That is when we can truly begin to impact and affect those around us.

I think of the famous lyrics by Louis Armstrong: "When you're smiling, the whole world smiles with you." Louis was obviously on to something, as science has proven those lyrics to be true.

Neuroscience has shown that merely seeing a smile (or a frown) activates mirror neurons in the brain that mimic the emotion. Translated: When someone smiles at us, we smile back. And vice versa.

If you're thinking this sounds a bit too much like a Hallmark card, think about it on a macro level, in terms of things such as peace and reconciliation. Whether it's the Israelis and Palestinians, the Rwandan Hutus and Tutsi, or the Serbs and Croatians, every effort at reconciliation needs a first step, a moment when one party reaches out, when one party makes an initial gesture of peace; in essence, when one party takes the initiative to smile. And that first step is what starts the healing.

And it's as powerful on a micro level. Let's say you have a deadline and a particularly needy coworker comes in to ask your help with something. And let's say that on that same day you are carrying a load of anger and resentment. Thanks to that baggage, you cut the poor coworker off abruptly and send her away. That person has now left your presence with your handprint—your baggage. She takes it out into the office, the community, the world, and shares it.

What if your handprint, however, were not anger and resentment, but joy? The ripple effects might be drastically different. How much more can you effect change in yourself and others if that simple smile grows into acts of compassion and kindness?

A smile is a handprint we all carry. With a simple choice of smiling rather than frowning, we can affect not only our own heart, but the quality of another's life as well. A smile is one of the most overlooked but powerful tools we have. It is the opportunity to change the world one smile at a time.

Just-In Time

> "Count your nights by stars not shadows; count your life with smiles, not tears."
>
> —ITALIAN PROVERB

One of my congregation members adopted a dog from the local shelter. It was a very cute Collie/Labrador Retriever mix that was within days of being euthanized. After the paperwork was done, she took him home and immediately named him "Just-in," for just-in-time.

Just-in's story is our story, too. Maybe you feel stuck in a dead-end job or a dying relationship. Or maybe you feel your dreams have faded or your sense of joy has disappeared. Many of us are walking this earth physically alive but dead of spirit, operating at the level of our social security number—existing, not living. And just like Just-in, our situation can change. But time is ticking.

The key to any change is taking one step at a time, one breath at a time, one prayer at a time. Too often we try to change ourselves, our environment, our world with sweeping transformations, when all along it is the little things done consistently that make the most change.

The Great Pyramids were built one brick at a time. The Great Wall of China—one brick at a time. Dollywood, the Mall of America, Graceland—all built one brick at a time.

In explaining his theory on climbing, Sir Edmund Hillary said that it's the same pattern over and over: "one whack of the ice-axe, one weary step." Those tiny steps, repeated for days on end, made him the first man to summit Mt. Everest.

> "It's never too late to be what you might have been."
>
> —George Eliot, English novelist

It's never too late. As a performer and comedian, I understand that the ending is always the most important part. You have to leave them with your best material. Even if you bombed in the beginning of the set, if you leave them laughing in the end, that's what they will remember.

Just like a comedian who teaches him or herself to "see" humor in the world, so too can you relearn to see the joy in everyday life. And no matter how you've lived to date, if that is how you end, that's what they'll remember.

It is important to know who you are. It is, however, more important to know who you are *becoming*. Ask yourself: "Do I want to be a resentful, angry, exhausted human being?" Then give priority to the "to-do" lists and the failures and money and power and the multitasking and the need to be right all the time. Or if your answer is that you want to leave a legacy as a loving, compassionate, peaceful human being, then show it. Give priority to compassion and patience and peace.

Err on the side of Tigger.

Smile.

At the end of the dash years, there is only one question each of us has to answer: Did we leave the world a better place?

What if this were your last day? You may have years left, but why risk it? If this were your last day, how would you live it?

The Buddhist teacher Thich Nhat Hanh said, "If in our daily life we can smile, if we can be peaceful and happy, not only we, but everyone will profit from it."

Take stock of how you spend your time. Think about the handprint you want to leave on the world—how others feel after being in your presence.

The most important thing on your tombstone is not the date you were born, or the date you died, but that "dash in between." And the best way—the only way—to truly honor this short legacy is one smile at a time, one laugh at a time, one joyful compassionate act at a time. Honor your gift of life and spirit. Smile, love, and laugh your way to grace.

REFLECTIONS

How's it going with your "dash in between?"

Are you predominantly an Eeyore or a Tigger? Do you smile more or complain more? How does that affect those around you? What would you like to change?

If you could write your own funeral eulogy, what would it say at this point in your life? What do you *want* it to say?

Find one tiny thing to smile or laugh about today. It doesn't matter what it is. Find it and share it with a friend or a loved one or even better with a stranger. At the end of your day, reflect on the joyful handprint you shared. Think about how it may have begun a tiny, but significant chain reaction—a healing for your community and for your world.

Suggestions for Further Reading

Books

Adams, Doug. *The Prostitute in the Family Tree: Discovering Humor and Irony in the Bible.* Louisville, KY: Westminster John Knox Press, 1997.

Cosby, Bill. *Bill Cosby Is a Very Funny Fellow, Right!* New York: Warner Brothers Records, 1963.

Cox, Harvey. *The Feast of Fools: A Theological Essay on Festivity and Fantasy.* New York: Harper & Row, 1969.

De Mello, Anthony. *Taking Flight.* New York: Doubleday, 1988.

Doskoch, Peter. "Happily Ever Laughter," *Psychology Today*, July 1, 1996, www.psychologytoday.com/articles/199607/happily-ever-laughter.

Freud, Sigmund. *Jokes and Their Relation to the Unconscious.* New York: W.W. Norton, 1960.

Griffin, R. Morgan. "Why We Laugh," WebMD, http://men.webmd.com/features/why-we-laugh.

Hample, Stuart, and Eric Marshall. *Children's Letters to God.* New York: Workman Publishing, 1991.

Humor Therapy Infocenter. "Introduction," Holisticonline.com, www.holisticonline.com/Humor_Therapy/humor_therapy_introduction.htm.

Hyers, M. Conrad, ed. *Holy Laughter: Essays on Religion in the Comic Perspective.* New York: The Seabury Press, 1969.

———. *The Laughing Buddha: Zen and the Comic Spirit.* Durango, CO: Longwood Academic, 1989.

Klein, Allen. *The Healing Power of Humor.* New York: Tarcher Putnam, 1989.

LaMott, Anne. *Grace (Eventually): Thoughts on Faith*. New York: Penguin, 2007.

Morreall, John. *Comedy, Tragedy, and Religion*. Albany: State University of New York Press, 1999.

Provine, Robert R. *Laughter: A Scientific Investigation*. New York: Viking Press, 2000.

Samra, Cal. *The Joyful Christ: The Healing Power of Humor*. San Francisco: HarperSanFrancisco, 1985.

Sanders, Barry. *Sudden Glory: Laughter as Subversive History*. Boston: Beacon Press, 1995.

Trueblood, Elton. *The Humor of Christ*. New York: Harper & Row, 1964.

Wooten, Patty. *Compassionate Laughter: Jest for Your Health*. Salt Lake City: Commune-a-Key Publishing, 1996.

Resources

Association for Applied and Therapeutic Humor
220 East State Street, Fl. G
Rockford, IL 61104
815-708-6587
www.aath.org

Clowns Without Borders—USA
PO Box 460523
San Francisco, CA 94146
603-724-4840 Tel / Fax
http://clownswithoutborders.org

The ComedyCures Foundation
122 East Clinton Avenue
Tenafly, NJ 07670
201-227-8410 Tel
888-300-3990 Tel
201-227-8411 Fax
www.ComedyCures.org

About SKYLIGHT PATHS Publishing

SkyLight Paths Publishing is creating a place where people of different spiritual traditions come together for challenge and inspiration, a place where we can help each other understand the mystery that lies at the heart of our existence.

Through spirituality, our religious beliefs are increasingly becoming a part of our lives—rather than *apart* from our lives. While many of us may be more interested than ever in spiritual growth, we may be less firmly planted in traditional religion. Yet, we do want to deepen our relationship to the sacred, to learn from our own as well as from other faith traditions, and to practice in new ways.

SkyLight Paths sees both believers and seekers as a community that increasingly transcends traditional boundaries of religion and denomination—people wanting to learn from each other, *walking together, finding the way.*

For your information and convenience, at the back of this book we have provided a list of other SkyLight Paths books you might find interesting and useful. They cover the following subjects:

Buddhism / Zen	Gnosticism	Poetry
Catholicism	Hinduism /	Prayer
Chaplaincy	Vedanta	Religious Etiquette
Children's Books	Inspiration	Retirement & Later-
Christianity	Islam / Sufism	Life Spirituality
Comparative	Judaism	Spiritual Biography
Religion	Meditation	Spiritual Direction
Earth-Based	Mindfulness	Spirituality
Spirituality	Monasticism	Women's Interest
Enneagram	Mysticism	Worship
Global Spiritual	Personal Growth	
Perspectives		

CPSIA information can be obtained
at www.ICGtesting.com
Printed in the USA
FSHW011951100122
87535FS